Inner City Regeneration

Inner City Regeneration

Robert K. Home PhD
Senior Lecturer in Planning Studies
North East London Polytechnic

LONDON NEW YORK
E. & F. N. Spon

First published 1982 by
E. & F.N. Spon Ltd
11 New Fetter Lane, London EC4P 4EE
Published in the USA by
E. & F.N. Spon
in association with Methuen, Inc.
733 Third Avenue, New York NY 10017

Typeset by Inforum Ltd, Portsmouth
Printed in Great Britain at the
University Press, Cambridge

ISBN 0 419 12150 1 (cased)
ISBN 0 419 12160 9 (paperback)

British Library Cataloguing in Publication Data

Home, Robert
Inner city regeneration.
1. Urban renewal—Great Britain
I. Title
711.4'0941 HT178.G72

ISBN 0-419-12150-1
ISBN 0-419-12160-9 Pbk

Contents

List of illustrations

Acknowledgments

I wish to thank the following for their help: my former colleagues at the London Borough of Hackney Planning Department, especially Mike New and John Burrow; John Overall, my head of department at North East London Polytechnic, for allowing me the freedom to get on with the book; the library staff of the Waltham Forest precinct (especially Ted Maloney); numerous busy officials of central government, local government and other institutions who talked to me; and my wife Olive.

September 1981 Robert Home

Introduction

The inner city debate emerged in Britain in the 1970s as a focus for bringing together a number of matters of public concern and remained important into the 1980s, particularly with the growth of riots and disorder in the inner city. These matters included urban deprivation and racial disadvantage, unemployment and industrial decline, the effects of past planning and dispersal policies, and the role of a newly-reformed local government. Social researchers thrown up by the expansion of higher education in the 1960s found the analysis of inner city problems a rich area for them to contribute to public policy-making. The Government White Paper, *Policy for the Inner Cities* 1977, presented inner city regeneration as an opportunity for a co-ordinated approach to economic and social problems. Inner city policy was therefore important as a means of extending corporate management thinking in central and local government.

The inner cities face many of the same problems that big cities have always faced, for example, slum housing, poverty, congestion, to mention a few; but a distinction between the central, inner and outer areas of conurbations has become necessary, as better jobs and more affluent people have moved out to the suburbs, new towns and elsewhere. Also certain new elements distinguish inner city problems from general urban problems. It was the racial aspect, as immigrants from the New Commonwealth formed new ethnic minority groups in British society with their particular problems of disadvantage and cultural friction, which first drew attention to the inner city. Subsequently the economic problems of the inner city have seemed to supplant their social problems in importance and urgency: the inner cities have experienced declines in population, economy and services with particular severity, as a result of decentralization, demographic trends, technological obsolescence and other factors. By the mid-1970s Government policies encouraging the dispersal of people and jobs from the cities had been revised, if not abandoned, and the urgent need for economic regeneration became dominant. This has created a difficulty with respect to definition: whether inner city policy is primarily concerned with the problems of the residents, or with the economic activity (or inactivity) of the inner areas.

That is only one of the difficulties of defining and analysing what the inner city is. A working definition might be: those zones of older (mainly 19th century) residential and industrial development, lying between the centres and suburbs of the major conurbations, where the physical, social and economic problems, usually called urban deprivation, are concentrated. However, selecting those cities or conurbations with a significant inner city dimension is not simple: the major British conurbations (inner London, Merseyside, Greater Manchester, West Midlands, West Yorkshire, Tyne-and-Wear, Clydeside) are included, although they do not correspond precisely with the six metropolitan counties created in England in the 1974 local government reorganization. Other cities are also usually included, such as Cardiff, Sheffield and Hull, but not the more prosperous cities of the south, like Bristol and Southampton. Smaller towns and cities may have similar problems, but, as the Inner City White Paper stated, 'there must be a particular emphasis on the inner areas of some of the big cities because of the scale and intensity of their problems and the rapidity of rundown in population and employment' (p. 2).

Drawing geographical boundaries and devising appropriate statistical measures also have their problems. For instance, the population census provides much of the relevant data, but tends to emphasize housing and residents' statistics, and geographical boundaries for data collection may vary between agencies (e.g. between employment exchange and local authority areas). An important study by Holtermann (1976) grouped 1971 census indicators of urban deprivation in order to identify areas of multiple deprivation, and found that the worst 5% of urban enumeration districts (EDs) were concentrated in the conurbations. Unfortunately inner areas are neither homogeneous nor uniformly bad, nor do they contain all the deprived people: there are more people suffering 'deprivation' outside than inside the conurbations, although they are obviously less geographically concentrated. Geographers have used definitions like Metropolitan Economic Labour Area and Standard Metropolitan Labour Area as a basis for analysis, but these do not distinguish between inner and outer areas sufficiently well: for instance, analysis based on metropolitan and outer metropolitan areas concentrates mainly on commuting patterns.

Furthermore, ideology and political judgments affect the selection and definition of problems. A radical argument, while concerned with the concept of territorial justice, might be that defining geographical areas of deprivation for analysis obscures the structure of social inequality, and that area-based action will never solve the structural problems which derive from the nature and historical development of capitalism. As radical commentators have written:

> The term 'inner city' has now become virtually meaningless . . . Its function in debate is essentially ideological and not descriptive; in many cases it is used as a pseudonym for the 'working class' . . . we will not resolve it (the inner city crisis) until there is a commitment to resolve the more basic contradictions which permit the continued concentration of private wealth and its inevitable consequence in the spatial segregation of rich and poor (Loney, pp. 162–3).

Because inner city regeneration involves complex social, economic, environmental and political issues, no profession or academic discipline can claim a monopoly over it. To list them alphabetically (but not to claim completeness), architects, economists, environmentalists, geographers, historians, planners, political scientists, sociologists and surveyors have all contributed to 'the inner city debate', which has become increasingly confused and formless. Although there may seem to be a surfeit of writings on the subject of inner cities, and a major change away from it in governmental priorities, nevertheless inner city issues remain relevant and important, symbolizing a wider upheaval in the economy and society as a whole. The problems set may be the wrong ones, and may be insoluble, but nevertheless in practice the major task of regenerating the inner cities' economy and society has been embarked upon and those are the issues with which this book is concerned.

The intention of this book is to describe what has been done to regenerate the inner city since it became a topic of public interest, and particularly since the publication in 1977 of the Inner City White Paper. This synoptic approach will mean some omissions and oversimplifications, but will try to cover the broad range of inner city issues, and to show how the selection and definition of those issues have changed over time.

1

The development of inner city policy

The inner city problem is a historical legacy left by Britain's imperial past, the Industrial Revolution and 19th century urbanization. It was identified as a major new concern of Government in the 1970s by a process of policy formulation which absorbed a number of urban, spatial and economic problems within the broadly defined inner city problem. This first chapter examines briefly British city development in the 19th and 20th centuries, and the emergence of the principal elements in the inner city problem. The creation of the Urban Programme in 1968 is then taken as the starting point for an account of the development of government thinking on inner cities, traced through Community Development Programmes, Inner Areas Studies and the Inner City White Paper 1977, to the new initiatives by Labour and Conservative Governments since 1977, and the growth of disorder after 1980.

The rise and fall of the industrial city

The origins of the inner city problem lie in the 19th century, when Britain experienced industrialization and urbanization on an unprecedented scale. The population of the nation grew nearly four times during that century, and the proportion of people living in towns with a population over 20 000 rose from 17 to 77%. Job opportunities brought migrants pouring into the cities, where

Figure 1 The congested industrial city. This photograph (Commercial Street, East London, 1907) shows the high-density buildings, mixed uses, and congestion of traffic and people that characterized the inner city until it began to empty in the mid-20th century.

they commonly worked long hours at physically demanding, low-paid jobs, and lived in overcrowded and insanitary rented rooms.

Figure 2 The inner city today. A typical street scene showing boarded-up vacant land, old buildings in poor condition, exposed gable ends left over by demolition, temporary buildings, office blocks, on-street parking, and few people.

The physical development of the cities was as dramatic as their population growth. Working class housing was built in great quantities but was often insufficient to meet the demand. It was usually cramped because of the difficulties of ensuring an adequate return on capital investment for the developers and the need for workers to be within walking distance of their work. The types of housing varied regionally: in northern towns back-to-backs (typically one room up, one room down, with no through ventilation) were built and in London, multi-storey tenements were constructed because of the pressure on land. The Industrial Revolution created bigger and more specialized work-places than before, for example, multi-storey mills for the textile and other industries, docks, warehouses and construction sites for the great civil engineering projects. New modes of transport were brought into the cities, clearing slums and displacing people in the process: these included canals, followed by the railway, followed by the growth of horse-drawn and then horseless road traffic.

An unprecedented development and improvement of public services also occurred in the 19th century industrial city, for example, water supply, cemeteries, sewers, refuse collection and street cleansing (a working horse produces up to seven tons of dung a year). Public buildings proliferated: hospitals, schools, baths, libraries and town halls. The first *Public Health Act*, passed in 1848, was followed by improved building and town planning controls, wider streets and lower densities of buildings. Towards the end of the century enterprising municipal authorities undertook the supply of gas, electricity and water, as well as housing for the working classes.

During the 20th century, by contrast, the industrial city, essentially a creation of the Victorian period, has been in decline. The population of Britain's major cities seems to have reached a peak in about 1940 and thereafter to have stabilized or declined, although the extent to which this decline affected the inner areas was little realized until after the 1971 census. The strains created by social and economic change have led to the inner city problem.

Perhaps the most significant factor in inner city decline has been the increased mobility of goods and people. The development of cheap mass travel – railway, underground, tram and bus – first allowed people to escape from the crowded inner areas to live in the suburbs and then in the third quarter of the century the rapid increase in the number of cars and other vehicles created further opportunities for mobility as well as using up inner city land for roads and car parks.

This improved transport and mobility led to the large-scale decentralization of jobs and people. Other contributory factors were the processes of industrial rationalization, the Government's commitment after the Second World War to dispersing employment to new towns and depressed regions, increased home ownership and building society policies favouring modern suburban housing, and the disruptions of slum clearance and redevelopment. This decentralization coincided with the post-war wave of immigration to Britain, particularly New Commonwealth workers drawn by the demand for labour in the 1950s: as the indigenous population moved out of the inner areas, ethnic minorities moved in, because there they could find cheap housing and a large job market.

By the 1970s the principal elements of the so-called inner city problem could be seen clearly and were recognized by the Inner City White Paper in 1977:

> Many of the inner areas surrounding the centres of our cities suffer . . . from economic decline, physical decay and adverse social conditions . . . The inner parts of our cities ought not to be left to decay. It would mean leaving large numbers of people to face a future of declining job opportunities, a squalid environment, deteriorating housing and declining public services.

Physically the inner city comprises 20th century redevelopment and the surviving parts of the 19th century industrial city. On the one hand, massive redevelopment, by both public and private sectors, has not provided the 'New Jerusalem' that socialist visionaries and planners had hoped for after the Second World War. On the other hand, the 19th century industrial city has left a legacy of buildings and infrastructure unsuitable for modern needs and which are expensive to renew or improve: e.g. warehouses and mills, churches and cemeteries, sewers and electricity stations. The physical form of the inner city is further complicated by a historical confusion of land ownership and uses.

The inner city also seems to be in social and economic decline. Employment is at the heart of the problem, with jobs disappearing, especially in manufacturing and traditional industries, and workers moving out for better prospects elsewhere. The inner city residents left behind suffer from poverty, deprivation, unemployment, disruptive redevelopment and racial disharmony, while the population and rate base is inadequate to improve their living conditions. As the Inner City White Paper stated:

> Some of the changes which have taken place are due to social and economic forces which could be reversed only with great difficulty or at unacceptable cost. But . . . it should be possible now to change the thrust of the policies which have assisted large-scale decentralization and in the course of time to stem

> the decline, achieve a more balanced structure of jobs and population within our cities, and create healthier local economies (p. 5).

The White Paper's analysis, however, failed to take sufficient account of the powerful forces of technological change, de-industrialization and economic recession, which, since it was written, have accelerated the decline of traditional manufacturing, the disappearance of jobs and changes in job skills, thus aggravating the inner city problem.

Towards an inner city policy

The development of government thinking on inner cities can be traced to the policy initiatives of the Labour Government of Harold Wilson (1964–70). 'Urban deprivation', although not always so called, has long been a topic of periodic public concern, reported on by social investigators like Mayhew, Booth and Rowntree. But the Second World War, post-war redevelopment and increased prosperity temporarily diverted attention in Britain from the ever-present problem of poverty. The Conservatives' slogan in the 1950s was 'You've never had it so good'. The Wilson government, the first Labour Government for twelve years, was concerned that people should have equality of access to the new opportunities and social researchers developed concepts like 'deprived areas' (seen as islands of poverty in the general sea of prosperity) and the 'cycle of poverty' (in which families or indeed whole communities transmitted cultural disadvantages from one generation to the next like a disease).

Attention was drawn to inner city problems by the issue of race and immigration. The non-white population of Britain was over half a million in 1966, approximately an eight-fold increase since the Second World War, and was largely concentrated in the inner areas. Following the introduction of immigration controls the Government began to realize that the new immigrant communities were experiencing acute problems of adjustment, particularly in housing, education and employment, and it was feared that the race riots of 1967–8 in the USA might also happen in Britain. The speeches of the then Conservative politician Enoch Powell envisaged racial conflict destroying the fabric of British society: 'Like the Romans, I seem to see the River Tiber foaming with much blood' (20 April 1968). The Wilson Government at the time was also worried about its loss of political support in Labour's traditional strongholds, the cities. Against this background the Government took three initiatives which were important in the development of inner city policy: educational priority areas, the urban programme and the community development programme.

The concept of educational priority areas (EPAs) originated with the Plowden Report, *Children and their Primary Schools* 1967. This was one of several Government reports which identified deprived areas, mainly in the inner cities, whose special needs required positive discrimination by Government in allocating resources. This area-based approach remained an important tool of inner city policy, applied to housing problems through different kinds of housing improvement areas, and more recently to economic problems through industrial improvement areas and enterprise zones. In the area-based approach, areas for special attention are identified by analysis and correlation of the available statistical indicators, a process aided by improved technologies for information-handling. Critics of the approach argue that the statistics themselves only identify that which can be measured, obscuring unquantifiable but significant factors, and that the problems of deprivation have deep structural causes which initiatives based on arbitrary geographical boundaries cannot affect.

In 1968 Prime Minister Wilson, responding to Powell's inflammatory speeches, and borrowing the idea from President Johnson's Poverty Programme in the USA, announced the setting up of an Urban Programme, intended in his words 'to deal with the problems of areas where immigration had been at a high rate'. The initial funding was to be £20–25 million over four years, and the statutory basis was the *Local Government Grants (Social Needs) Act* 1969, with the Home Office taking the main coordinating role. Until the Urban Programme arrangements were changed in 1977, several thousand projects, proposed by local authorities and voluntary organizations, were approved. The emphasis was on capital rather than recurring expenditure, on experimental or innovative projects supplementing main programmes, and on educational projects like pre-school playgroups.

There seems to have been little systematic setting of objectives, nor much analysis of relative priorities or of the geographical distribution of projects, with the result that some local authorities were proportionately overfunded or underfunded relative to their degree of deprivation.

The third initiative was the Community Development Project (CDP), begun in 1969 as 'a neighbourhood-based experiment aimed at finding new ways of meeting the needs of people living in areas of high social deprivation' (Home Secretary Callaghan speaking in Parliament).

Twelve local projects, with a central team at the Home Office, were established in suitably deprived neighbourhoods with populations of 10 000–20 000, mostly in inner areas. Each project ran for about five years, with project teams affiliated to a local centre of higher education. The emphasis was on improving the co-ordination and responsiveness of local services, and on 'action research', whereby the researchers sought to involve themselves in community organizations. As the projects developed, the local teams not only clashed with their sponsoring local authorities, but increasingly criticized the Home Office's apparent assumption that poverty results from a social pathology, the 'cycle of poverty', which can be eradicated. Their experience and research, particularly on the history of industrial politics in their areas, led them to a more radical view, seeing deprivation initiatives as 'not about eradicating poverty at all, but managing poor people . . . The basic dilemma for the state remains the same – how best to respond to the needs of capital on the one hand and maintain the consent of the working class on the other' (*Gilding the Ghetto*, p. 63). This structural conflict view of society was too much for the Home Office, which closed down the CDP in 1977 with no official final report. The CDP workers produced the independent report, *Gilding the Ghetto*, with the disclaimer that 'This report does not necessarily reflect the views of the Home Office or any of the local authorities'.

The Conservative Government of Edward Heath succeeded Wilson from 1970 to 1974. The newly created Department of the Environment, a merger of three ministries, under its Secretary of State, Peter Walker, began to take the initiative on urban problems away from the Home Office, although the latter did establish an Urban Deprivation Unit in 1973 and the Comprehensive

Community Programme experiments in 1974. Walker, influenced by the rise of community-based groups, particularly the Shelter Neighbourhood Action Project (SNAP) in Liverpool, began to advocate a 'total approach' to urban problems, and in the *Making Towns Better* studies in 1972–3 commissioned management consultants to examine three northern towns and advise how to develop this approach. While these reports influenced the management style of local government, which was reorganized in 1974, more important in the evolution of inner city policy were the Inner Area Studies prepared between 1972 and 1977.

In these studies planning consultants worked on three inner areas: Small Heath, Birmingham (Llewelyn-Davies, Weeks, Forestier-Walker and Bor); Stockwell, south London (Shankland Cox Partnership with the Institute of Community Studies); and Liverpool, Merseyside (Hugh Wilson and Lewis Womersley, with two other consultant firms). The Department of the Environment gave them four instructions: to suggest definitions for inner areas and their problems; to experiment with environmental improvements; to investigate the concept of area management; and to provide a basis for conclusions on statutory powers, resources and techniques. The consultants combined the action research approach of the CDPs with environmental improvements and other projects. All provided lengthy final reports as well as numerous interim reports and studies. The consultants' final reports were summarized in a Department of the Environment publication, *Inner Area Studies: Liverpool, Birmingham and Lambeth* 1977.

The Liverpool study emphasized 'a total approach towards the inner area which would build up a comprehensive understanding of its problems, and take concerted action for their solution' (*Summary*, p. 12). This total approach would be pursued through four programmes: '(a) promoting the economic development of inner Liverpool; (b) expanding opportunities for training; (c) improving access to housing for disadvantaged groups of people and (d) channelling resources to areas of greatest social need' (p. 9).

The Birmingham study states that 'if downward trends are to be reversed and inner area residents are to be given opportunities more comparable to those of people elsewhere, the underlying problems of incomes, employment and housing must be tackled as the first priority. Next in importance is the problem of improving Government's performance – its sensitivity to needs and its efficient and economic delivery of services' (p. 21). On employment the study defined three 'crucial points':

> (a) The greatest cause of the extremely rapid loss of manufacturing jobs has been not the movement of firms but their death, and to a lesser extent, the small number of births of new firms to replace those dying.
> (b) Much the largest part of this loss has been due to the death of large establishments, which have closed because of trading changes; the loss of jobs in small firms has been less important in aggregate terms, though it has been exacerbated by the effects of planning policies and redevelopment.
> (c) Employment is very vulnerable to changes in trading conditions in the economy (p. 23).

On housing the study identified three problems:

> (a) The avoidable human misery that has been involved in the process of redevelopment and in Birmingham's extensive use of short-life housing.
> (b) The failure of housing resources to reach people and houses in greatest need.
> (c) The imbalance in investment between new construction and rehabilitation (p. 25).

The study went on to suggest ways of improving local government's sensitivity to problems through area committees, community organizations and by more emphasis on flexible planning with devices like area community plans and community reviews. It ended with a plea for urgent action: 'The most important short-term objective is to restore the confidence of residents and potential investors in the future of inner areas. What is essential is that action to set revitalization under way is taken – now, while retrieval is still possible' (p. 35).

The Lambeth study adopted a more heretical approach with its policy of 'balanced dispersal'. It concluded:

> (a) As well as measures to strengthen inner London's employment base and improve training measures, an essential part of policy must be to help low-skill people to move where the jobs are increasingly found.

(b) Since many people want to move out of inner London anyway, a scheme for balanced dispersal will have no shortage of applicants. It will arrest the social bi-polarization of inner London.

(c) Balanced dispersal will make it possible to reduce densities among those who stay behind, and generally to improve housing conditions and the local environment.

(d) A parallel policy of encouraging population stability among those who remain, helped by the abandonment of wholesale clearance and its substitution by more selective small-scale rehabilitation and development, will contribute to better relations between residents and more effective informal control of vandalism and petty crime.

(e) More sensitive housing management, resident caretakers supported by better maintenance and cleaning services, fuller involvement by tenants, and housing designed to a more human scale will all help to improve the quality of inner city life.

(f) A new Government programme, giving extra help to inner areas where deprived people are concentrated, will ensure that more resources are available locally. Improved access from below, boundary co-ordination and the creation of multi-service teams will lead to a more effective delivery of services and a more efficient use of resources (pp. 47–8).

The studies were criticized on various grounds, particularly for their piecemeal and academic approach. They were nevertheless influential in formulating a new inner city policy. All the studies stressed that inner city problems resulted from major structural changes in the economy and in the functions of the cities, and that employment opportunities must be improved in any new Government initiative.

The arrival of inner city policy

The Government White Paper, *Policy for the Inner Cities* (the Inner City White Paper), issued in July 1977, marked off the urban policy experiments of the previous decade from the new initiatives, and was a major commitment by the Labour Governments of Wilson and Callaghan (1974–9).

In September 1976 Peter Shore, Secretary of State for the Environment, became chairman of a ministerial committee on urban affairs, an appointment which reflected the transfer of responsibility for inner city problems away from the Home Office, and in a series of major speeches Shore outlined the new policy. In February 1977 the growing public concern with inner city decline was articulated in the *Save Our Cities* conference at Bristol, sponsored by the *Sunday Times* and Gulbenkian Foundation, at which Shore summarized the main contents of the White Paper shortly to be published.

The White Paper proposed, as the underlying aims of inner city policy: '(a) Strengthening the economies of the inner areas and the prospects of their residents; (b) improving the physical fabric of the inner areas and making their environment more attractive; (c) alleviating social problems; and (d) securing a new balance between the inner areas and the rest of the city region in terms of population and jobs' (p. 6). The White Paper, drawing on the conclusions of the CDP and Inner Area Studies, stated that 'the decline in the economic fortunes of the inner areas often lies at the heart of the problem' (p. 2), and emphasized incentives to industry and changes in industrial location policy. Local government was one of Shore's ministerial responsibilities and local authorities were identified as 'the natural agencies to tackle inner area problems' (p. 8), although contributions were invited from private sector investment and voluntary groups. The Urban Programme, responsibility for which was transferred from the Home Office to the Department of the Environment, was to be expanded from £30 million to £125 million per annum in the 1979–80 financial year, and emphasis was placed on redirecting the much larger main expenditure programmes of public authorities. An annex to the White Paper set out policy changes to assist the inner areas in the fields of housing, land, derelict land, planning, environment, education, social services, health and transport.

The main experiment in the White Paper was the special partnership arrangement, between central government, local government and some other public authorities in certain areas, funded from the Urban Programme. The guiding ideas behind the partnerships were defined as the need to concentrate resources, the need for co-ordinated action because of the complexity of the problems and the need to tailor policies and action to local requirements. To avoid the seven partnerships monopolizing inner city resources, 15 local authorities were designated as 'programme authorities' and allocated Urban Programme funds, although less than the partnerships. Chapter 7 gives further details of the workings of partnerships.

Outside England, Britain's inner city and deprivation problems also exist in Scotland (mainly Glasgow), Wales (mainly Cardiff and the valleys of South Wales), and Northern Ireland (mainly Belfast). All of these have classic inner city problems, with declining economies based upon ports and heavy industry, but owing to their historically different systems of government, the arrangements for putting inner city policies into effect vary. In Scotland the Glasgow Eastern Area Renewal (GEAR) project had already anticipated the inner city partnerships as a co-ordinated, comprehensive approach to inner city regeneration, and Urban Programme resources were enlarged. The Secretary of State for Wales had responsibility for the Urban Programme there, and a number of authorities in South Wales took advantage of inner city policy, particularly the *Inner Urban Areas Act* 1978. In Northern Ireland, while Belfast has the highest unemployment and the worst housing stock of any British city, identifying a specifically inner city dimension to its problems is of minor political significance compared to its violent Protestant–Catholic sectarian rivalries and its constitutional status in relation to Great Britain and the Irish Republic. Also the additional resources which a new inner city policy might provide are small compared to the massive levels of Government assistance, particularly special regional development grants, which Northern Ireland already receives.

In the two years between the White Paper and the fall of the Labour Government in May 1979, partnership and programme authorities were the main agents of inner city policy through their Inner Area Programmes, funding for which was maintained and even increased in spite of the national economic difficulties. Those economic difficulties made employment creation and economic regeneration increasingly important in the Inner Area Programmes and in other Government activities, such as the Manpower Services Commission and the industrial strategy. Dispersal policies which successive Governments had applied since the Second World War were partially dismantled, notably by setting lower financial allocations and growth targets for the new towns. In 1978 the *Inner Urban Areas Act* was passed, which empowered local authorities to declare industrial or commercial improvement areas and give financial assistance to companies; this followed from the activities of enterprising authorities like Rochdale and Tyne-and-Wear.

The manifestos of the main political parties for the 1979 general election showed what importance (if any) they gave to inner city issues, and their perception of the key national issues indicated the flavour of the different party ideologies and the likely effect on inner city policy. For the Conservatives, the key issues were to restore the health of economic and social life, restore incentives, uphold Parliament and the rule of law, support family life and strengthen national defence; for Labour they were to curb inflation, improve industrial relations, restore full employment, enlarge people's freedom, strengthen world peace and defeat world poverty. The Labour Party referred specifically to 'The Inner City' as one of the forty topics in its manifesto and stressed bringing jobs back to these areas as well as spending more on 'refurbishment, education, housing and social services', but immediately afterwards sought to restore the balance by a topic headed 'Rural Areas'. The Conservative Party manifesto did not include the inner city in its forty topics, but did refer indirectly to inner city issues in its sections on small firms (removing planning restraints), deterring the criminal, race relations (more English language training in schools and factories), sale of council houses, reviving the private sector and protecting the environment (including derelict land restoration). It was reasonable to expect, therefore, much less commitment to inner city policy if the Conservatives won the election, not least because of their low level of support in those areas. The Liberal Party manifesto also did not include the inner city, but did stress the importance of 'safeguarding the environment'.

When the Conservative Government took power, the new Secretary of State for the Environment, Michael Heseltine, reasserted the Government's concern with the inner city problem and support for the partnership and programme authority arrangements. Subsequent cuts in Government spending, however, eroded the ability of local government to tackle inner city problems in the way the White Paper had hoped, by redirecting their own main programmes, to such an extent that some felt the inner

Figure 3 After the riots. Upper Parliament Street, in the Toxteth area of Liverpool, showing the sites where buildings damaged in the 1981 riots have been demolished. Anglican Cathedral in the background.

city policy was being abandoned. Heseltine exhorted a reluctant private sector to assume a greater role in redeveloping and regenerating the inner city, for instance by encouraging the release of unused public land for private development. Enterprise zones were created as experiments in 'laissez faire', to release the private sector from allegedly stifling regulations and financial burdens. The new Government's other innovation was to establish Urban Development Corporations for the London and Merseyside docklands, on the model of new town development corporations, an idea which the Labour Government had considered and rejected.

In the spring and summer of 1981 riots and disorder in many inner areas, notably Toxteth (Liverpool), Brixton (London), and Moss-side (Manchester), gave a new urgency to the inner city problem. The outbreak of shop-looting, arson of banks and other buildings, and violent exchanges with the police, was attributed to various causes, among them over-aggressive policing (especially to the West Indians of Brixton), chronic high youth unemployment, and frustration at the ineffectiveness of inner city policies over more than a decade. The Home Office appointed Lord Justice Scarman to investigate the Brixton riots, and Environment Secretary Heseltine, after visiting the disturbed areas of Liverpool, modified inner city policies, mainly by increasing central government involvement in co-ordinating spending and attracting private investment.

Conclusions

After ten years of research and experiment, inner city policy emerged as a distinct area of government activity with the Inner City White Paper in 1977. A number of aspects to this development can be stressed.

Firstly, the dominant concerns of inner city policy have shifted, from social problems (urban deprivation, cycles of poverty and immigrant adjustment) to economic and physical problems (industrial decline, environmental decay, the small-firm sector and promotion of development), largely as a result of the analyses made by the Inner Areas Studies. The transfer of main responsibility for urban problems from the Home Office to the Department of the Environment in 1976–7 reflected this shift in emphasis, as did the four subsequent inner city initiatives: partnerships, industrial improvement areas, enterprise zones and urban development corporations. The riots after 1980 emphasized the importance of economic decline and unemployment in undermining social order.

Secondly, the agencies expected to take the lead in solving inner city problems changed, from the public to the private sector, and, more specifically, from local government to a mixed-sector approach. Central government, unable or unwilling to intervene directly itself, in the Inner City White Paper saw the task of inner city regeneration as a challenge for the newly reformed local authorities, responding to their local problems with the new skills of corporate management and public participation. When financial constraints dramatically reduced the contribution that local government could make, private enterprise was invoked to take on the task, although its response was less than enthusiastic.

Thirdly, because of resource limitations, and, to a certain

extent, the limited definition and analysis of the problems, Government programmes have emphasized area-based improvements and experimental or pump-priming projects. From the 1960s the Plowden Report and other policy and research reports had advocated that limited resources should be concentrated on the worst areas, since resources were insufficient for a comprehensive solution to the problems. Housing and industrial improvement areas, and inner city partnerships, are examples of this 'worst first' approach, which has not been particularly successful. The Urban Programme, the Inner City Programme which derived from it and other government financial programmes have, for similar reasons, encouraged experimental or demonstration projects. These offer more financial flexibility than large-scale Government projects and usually involve voluntary and community organizations, but their combined effect on the major structural problems of the inner city seems to have been marginal.

Fourthly, inner city policy resulted from a predominantly middle class analysis of working class problems, and has been a means of damping down the potential threat to law and order from poor or deprived people. Until the Inner City White Paper most specific inner city government spending went on research by academics and consultants (the most expensive being the Inner Areas Studies). Identifying and analysing problems seems to have attracted at least as much resources as direct action to solve problems, or, in crude words, middle class social science researchers have earned more out of 'the inner city problem' than deprived inner city residents are likely to. The benefits of the Inner City Programme seem to have accrued more to the better-off than the worse-off inner city residents, and particularly to have done little for those ethnic minorities whose problems had been of urgent concern in the early days of inner city policy. Recent private enterprise activity has unsurprisingly emphasized the profitable rather than the socially desirable. 'Positive discrimination' seems to have failed or at least failed to attract extra resources, as the disorders after 1980 emphatically showed.

2

The agencies for inner city regeneration

The massive and complex task of inner city regeneration, if achievable at all, requires more than a policy commitment by Government. The Inner City White Paper (1977) discussed 'the agencies for action' under the headings 'public authorities' (particularly the local authorities, which it called 'the natural agencies to tackle inner area problems'), 'local communities and voluntary bodies' and the 'rôle of the private sector'. This chapter examines the role of the main agencies.

Central government

Central government's direct role as an agent of inner city regeneration is limited. The 1977 Inner City White Paper remains its principal policy statement on the subject, although that hardly reflects a pure and coherent policy, but rather the result of the incremental approach adopted over the previous decade.

Chapter 1 referred to the role of central government in commissioning research studies to inform policy-making, and also to the changes in policy emphasis resulting from realignments between central government departments (notably the shift of control of inner city policy from the Home Office to the Department of the Environment). There now appears to be broad party agreement on inner city policy (with the exception of housing and land aspects), to such an extent that a recent study of urban politics categorized it as having 'virtually no party role or party differences. Low electoral salience' (MacKay and Cox, p. 265). Central government has exhorted other agencies to implement inner city policy, particularly through its circulars to local government, but it has limited power to compel them.

Inner city policy has led to some new legislation. The *Inner Urban Areas Act* 1978 gave increased powers to inner city authorities to assist industry and commerce, but was a modest policy response to the issue of economic regeneration. Some local authorities, notably the Tyne-and-Wear County Council, have increased their statutory powers to tackle inner city problems. The Conservative Government after 1979 passed the *Housing Act* 1980, which introduced short-hold tenancies and increased Council tenants' rights. The *Local Government, Planning and Land Act* 1980 had a number of major provisions affecting inner city issues. These included tighter controls over direct labour organizations (Part III), rating changes, a new system of domestic rate relief grants and block grants for rate support (Part VI), changes to town and country planning (Part IX), register of public authority owned underused land (Part X), repeal of the *Community Land Act* 1976 (Part XI), creation of Urban Development Corporations (Part XVI) and Enterprise Zones (Part XVIII). Apart from new laws, some modifications to regulatory statutory instruments have reflected inner city policy concerns, e.g. in town planning and in regional development grants.

The Inner City White Paper spoke of a 'co-ordinated approach to urban problems' (a watered-down version of Walker's 'total approach'), and this requires more co-ordination in central government: 'the activities of central government have themselves at times been over-compartmentalized' (p. 8). Since the 1960s corporate planning, originating in the USA and seeking a more unified and systematic approach to public policy-making and resource allocation, has become more influential in central government, notably through the Public Expenditure Service Committee (PESC) and Programme Analysis Review (PAR) systems. Inner city policy should, at least in theory, be a suitable testing ground for such an approach, but it has not happened in practice. Central government is organized functionally, and the inner city need only form part of a ministry's national concern: for instance, the Urban Programme in the early 1970s was co-ordinated and administered by one relatively small section of the Home Office, and in 1977, when it was announced that £125 million would be spent on the inner city programme, total Government expenditure was some £50 000 million. Co-ordinating and informing the activities of the departments most involved in inner city policy is only a small part of the transaction of central government's business, and views of priorities and definitions differ between and within departments, and also between the civil servants and the politicians. A summary of the main central government departments and their responsibilities most relevant to inner cities illustrates the difficulty of achieving a co-ordinated approach to inner city problems in central government:

(a) The Department of the Environment, with main responsibility for inner city policy (especially relations with local government) since 1977. One of the largest government ministries, created in 1970 in a merger of the Ministry of Housing and Local Government and two other ministries.

(b) The Home Office, responsible for law and order, race and community relations, losing interest in urban deprivation in recent years.

(c) The Department of Employment, responsible for employment exchanges and job centres, monitoring unemployment levels and employment promotion.

(d) The Department of Health and Social Security, responsible for the three-tier National Health Service (including the Resources Allocation Working Party) and for National Insurance and social security payments.

(e) The Department of Industry, responsible for regional development grants to industry and for Industrial Development Certificates.

(f) The Department of Transport, carved out from the Department of the Environment in 1976, responsible for national transport policy, including financial and policy control of the transport aspects of local government.

(g) The Department of Education and Science, responsible for central control of local education authorities, and for further and higher education.

To this list should be added: the 'Quangos' (quasi-autonomous national governmental organizations), such as the Commission for Racial Equality, the Housing Corporation and the Manpower Services Commission; the regional offices (the Scottish and Welsh Offices with their own ministers and different systems of government, and the decentralized government offices, particularly of the Department of the Environment and the Department of Industry); and the nationalized industries (particularly British Rail, gas and electricity).

The difficulty of achieving a co-ordinated inner city policy is reflected in central government spending programmes. Apart from the Inner City Programme, which is included in the Department of the Environment's financial allocation and shared with the local and health authorities involved, central government has not distinguished an inner city dimension in its financial plans. However, changes in the distribution of Government expenditure, and particularly reductions in public spending forced by adverse economic conditions, can affect the inner city situation drastically, for all the desires expressed in White Papers that the adverse effects on them be mitigated.

Deprived areas seem to suffer most from cuts. The study by Tunley, Travers and Pratt (1979) of education in an inner London borough showed, for instance, how spending cuts affected schools in the poorer and more deprived areas more than other schools. The regional redistribution of health service finance through the Resources Allocation Working Party (RAWP) seems to have reduced the service to residents of deprived areas of inner London. Tighter control of social security payments affects income levels in inner areas more because their residents have a higher dependence on such payments than elsewhere. With capital programmes often easier to cut than revenue, the construction industry has long been a hostage to the Government's financial decisions, and the inner cities have suffered particularly from the drop in housing investment programme targets.

Of the various central government departments, the most active in inner city policy have been the Manpower Services Commission, with responsibility for special employment creation programmes (examined in more detail in Chapter 4), and the Department of the Environment. Within the Department of the Environment a new Inner Cities Directorate was created in 1976–7, which had a staff of fifty in 1980 and responsibility for all aspects of inner city policy (including the traditional Urban Programme), while the regional offices of the Department of the Environment were also responsible for partnership, programme authority and enterprise zone arrangements in their regions. The Department of the Environment's responsibilities for the local government sector, and particularly for central–local financial relations, have also become a crucially important aspect of the inner city problem.

Central–local financial relations were examined by the Layfield Committee Report on Local Government Finance in 1976, and two aspects of those relations have particular relevance to the inner city situation: the calculation of Rate Support Grant (RSG) and the move to a corporate planning style of block grant. The dependence of local government on central funds has grown, until the RSG has become a more important source of local government income than the rates; and that grant includes a needs element, calculated by central government through a complex formula applying computerized regression analysis to a range of statistical indicators. The calculation of RSG acquired political importance in the 1970s when the 1974 Labour Government pledged to redistribute RSG in favour of the cities; the shire counties protested that they were being unfairly penalized. Following this the 1979 Conservative Government pledged to curtail local government over-spending, often in the same cities. The formula for calculating the needs element has been adjusted, notably by including unemployment levels and actual local spending patterns in the calculation. Metropolitan authorities after 1974 benefited from increased central government financial support, which helped avert the financial disasters that American city governments, notably New York, experienced at that time of major economic recession and inflation, but then the partial withdrawal of that support after 1979 created a new financial crisis for them. The London Borough of Tower Hamlets (which includes the constituency of Peter Shore, Secretary of State for the Environment at the time of the Inner City White Paper) was losing more money in 1974–7 from the redistribution of RSG than it gained from the Inner City Programme. A researcher, Travers, said:

The Government is not necessarily conspiring to deprive inner

> areas of support. But the use of technical changes to improve the accuracy of the distribution and to move the grant from one set of authorities to another, has led to baffling complexity. Mr Shore has probably thought that resources were being diverted to the areas he wanted to receive them. But he has been hoodwinked by the belief that if a distributive method is complex and statistically plausible, it is necessarily better than a simple solution (*The Guardian*, 17 November 1978).

The other aspect of central–local relations important to the inner cities is the move to a corporate planning style of block grant. Influenced by the Bains Report (1972) on the management of the new local authorities, the Department of the Environment encouraged a number of local authorities to experiment with corporate planning, and particularly planned programmed budgeting systems (PPBS). The Inner City Programme was used as a further means to advance corporate management in partnership authorities. The Department of the Environment has introduced new financial programming arrangements in the main areas of local government activity: the model is a programme of proposed expenditure, annually reviewed and rolled forward, usually over a five-year period, with policy information to support the programmes, prepared according to guidelines supplied by central government, and submitted to central government as a basis for grant approval. Transport Policies and Programmes, Social Service Plans, Housing Investment Programmes and Partnership Urban Programmes all follow this model, as did the short-lived Land Policy Statements under the *Community Land Act* 1976.

The *Local Government, Planning and Land Act* 1980 extended the block grant system over the whole area of local government rate support. This enabled central government to control the level of local government spending, particularly its share of the public sector borrowing requirement (PSBR), more closely than before, while offering individual local authorities ostensibly more freedom of choice on how to spend within the overall allocation. In setting the level of block grant the Secretary of State takes account of the rate of local authority expenditure, fluctuations in demand for services, the need to develop services in relation to 'general economic conditions', and the 'current level of prices, costs and remuneration'. The new system affected inner city local authorities more than others, because of their high spending on services and high congestion costs but falling population and rate base. The resources were drastically redistributed from the predominantly Labour-controlled inner cities to the predominantly Conservative-controlled shire counties. The dramatic inner city riots after 1980 did, however, show the dangers of such a redistribution, and helped re-establish inner city authorities' claim for special support.

The withholding of grant and other financial restrictions were part of a tighter control by central government over local government, and the disorders after 1980 contributed to increased central government involvement in the inner cities. Dependence of those areas on the MSCs special programmes to create jobs grew, in spite of the original intention that these would be only a temporary measure. After the riots of 1981 the Department of the Environment considered increasing its intervention in the inner cities, particularly by making a Minister and a central government directorate responsible for each major inner city, to coordinate central government spending, and also by dismantling the higher tier of city government, the metropolitan county councils.

Central government regulates the finance, not only of local government, but also of other public authorities, and the under-resourcing of their capital programmes has contributed to inner city decline, as a few examples show. Gas and electricity boards have withdrawn plant and investment from the inner areas, mainly to rationalize their operations, and have thus added their redundant premises to the vacant land and dereliction of the inner city. The water supply pipes and sewers in inner areas were often originally installed in the 19th century, when labour and materials were cheaper than they are now, and they are now antiquated and outworn, which leads to frequent burst mains and sewer collapses. Such 'underground dereliction' calls for large-scale renewal, but the capital resources of Water Authorities have been drastically cut in recent years. The public reaction against urban motorways has contributed to drastic cuts in road construction and maintenance programmes, and rail and public transport have also suffered severely.

Central government through various agencies can grant-aid

individual projects. The Urban Programme, the Inner City Programme, the Manpower Services Commission's special programmes and Regional Development Grants have the largest sources of such funds, running to hundreds of millions of pounds, but there are other sources, usually grants calculated as a percentage of eligible capital expenditure, subject to a maximum grant limit. Grant-giving bodies include: the English Tourist Board (for projects in the Assisted Areas), the Historic Buildings Council (on behalf of the Department of the Environment), the Arts Council (for professional artistic activities, through its Housing the Arts Fund), the Sports Council (particularly for local community projects in areas of special need), the Civic Trust (on behalf of the Department of the Environment, for projects in conservation areas), and the Department of the Environment for derelict land reclamation and other miscellaneous grants. Central government also handles grant applications to the European Economic Community, of which the European Regional Development Fund and the European Social Fund in particular have aided some inner city projects.

Local government

The Inner City White Paper identified local authorities as the main agents for implementing inner city policy. This reflected the growth in importance of the local government sector, and central government's wish to see it more actively directing and responding to change. But in practice the local authorities have not been able to achieve as much as was hoped, for a variety of reasons.

Local government's share of gross domestic product grew from 9% in 1949 to 12% in 1974, and the growth in staff and services was particularly marked in inner city authorities. The new local government system created in 1974, following the Maud Report (1969) and the *Local Government Act* 1972, replaced local authorities in England and Wales with a two-tier system of counties and districts. In the six English conurbations outside London, the system already used for London local government since 1965 was adopted of a metropolitan county council with up to ten metropolitan district councils, even though former city councils and county boroughs resented being subordinated for the first time to a higher tier of local government. Scottish local government was reorganized into a similar system, of regional and district councils, in 1975, with Glasgow and the Clydeside conurbation coming under the Strathclyde Region. Gas and electricity undertakings had long been removed from local authority control and nationalized, and water supply followed with the creation of regional water authorities under the *Water Act* 1973, while the health services were reorganized into regional, area and district health authorities under the *National Health Service Act* 1973. The new system was criticized for fragmentation and possible institutional instability, and has been modified since, notably by the abolition of area health authorities and by the *Organic Change* White Paper (Command 7547, 1979). That White Paper changed district–county relations and returned some powers to the former county boroughs, restive at their loss of power in the two-tier system. A more drastic change proposed was the total abolition of the metropolitan county councils as superfluous and wasteful.

Reorganization and inner city problems have demanded improved management in local authorities. Since the Bains Report (1972) local authorities have increasingly adopted a corporate management style, which involves the appointment of chief executives and management teams, new committee and organizational structures, the division of local authority activities into programme areas, improved information and programming systems, and new methods of public participation. In the *Making Towns Better* studies of three northern towns (Rotherham, Sunderland and Oldham) commissioned by the Department of the Environment in 1972–3, management consultants advised local authorities on how to achieve a 'total approach' to the urban environment, and the later Inner Area Studies also experimented with management techniques. Metropolitan authorities have tended to be the main experimenters in corporate planning and management, sometimes using management consultants to introduce the new approach, and inner city areas have often become laboratories for testing the new management techniques. Traditionally much local government activity has been preventive and regulatory (e.g. planning and public health controls), but the new management style and the nature of inner city problems require a more innovative and permissive approach. Unfortunately, encouraging diversity and experimentation may be incompatible with maintaining standards, a conflict which can inhibit the role of local government in inner city regeneration.

Political sociologists have criticized the new management style as being an extension of social control by the state. Local government officials are seen as 'urban gate-keepers', who control by their complex allocation procedures inner city residents' access to benefits like housing, social services and even employment. Local elected representatives have limited political supervision over this process, the complexities of which are poorly understood by themselves and the electorate they represent. The new urban managerialism identifies certain social 'problems' which it offers to 'solve' for individual people or for geographical areas like the inner cities and housing improvement areas; but it obscures structural conflicts in society, and particularly the crisis in the capitalist system which has created the social distress conveniently called the inner city problem. 'The connection between social problems and social order is reciprocal and planners as consumers of official definitions of social problems are placed in the position of being agents of the maintenance of such a social order' (Bailey, p. 141).

Local authorities in inner cities also have problems of democratic accountability and community involvement. While Britain has a high proportion of councillors to electorate compared with other countries, voting is generally poor in local elections (perhaps a third or less of those eligible to vote do so), and the political issues may seem irrelevant to the immediate problems of inner city residents. The popular reaction against the social disruption of urban redevelopment in the late 1960s has led to new attempts to involve the public in the processes of urban government. Party political differences between the two local government tiers, and between local and central government, sometimes complicate inner city policy further. Generally inner city district councils and Parliamentary constituencies are under Labour Control, but metropolitan county councils may have Conservative majorities because their areas also include the suburbs. Housing policy is a particular area of conflict, with a Conservative-controlled Greater London Council, for instance, seeking to promote owner-occupation by selling council houses to tenants and disposing of its land for private housing development, while the mainly Labour-controlled inner London boroughs contending that such policies will reduce the choice available to those in worst housing need.

The success of local authorities as the main agents for implementing inner city policy depends upon financial resources. The Inner City Programme, set in 1977 at £125 million, is tiny compared with total local government spending of some £18 000 million in that year, and therefore central government expected the local authorities to redirect or 'bend' their main programmes to achieve inner city policy objectives. Unfortunately for this anticipated role, local government spending fell in real terms by 15% between 1974 and 1980, mainly because of central government cuts in RSG and loan sanction. Inner city authorities have been particularly hard hit, because, while the distribution of RSG has favoured metropolitan areas, it seems that the structure of local government finance is biased in favour of suburban and against the inner areas. In Greater London, for instance, rate equalization procedures, designed to redistribute the high income from central London commercial premises, have apparently given outer London more money than the inner area boroughs, partly because of the complicated system of rating houses. The loss of population and business from the inner city tends to reduce taxable income and capital faster than the cost of providing urban public services, thus further penalizing inner city authorities. These authorities commonly have a declining population and rate base, so that large rate increases are needed when other sources of income fall, thus incurring the hostility of the rate-payers. To show the decline of rateable values, in five English conurbations the total rateable value of the inner areas as a proportion of the rateable value of the conurbations fell by an average of over 3% between 1966 and 1973, and the penny rate product expressed as a similar proportion over the same period fell by nearly 3% (Kennett, 1980).

Cumbersome local government financial procedures add to the difficulties, since the system of annual estimates, standing orders and audit controls has hindered speedy implementation of the many small-scale projects associated with inner city regeneration. Often funds have not been fully spent in the time they were available, and it is difficult to plan and implement schemes when financial allocations fluctuate between and even within accounting years.

Local authority staffing establishments make an important

contribution to employment in the inner cities, particularly through their direct labour organizations (DLOs), which carry out council house building and other construction and maintenance work. But along with the general fall in local government staffing levels, the *Local Government, Planning and Land Act* 1980 has increased restrictions on DLO accounting and tendering procedures. Under the new rules DLOs must bid for a substantial proportion of their work against competitive tenders from the private sector, must earn a prescribed rate of return on capital (set initially at 5% by the Secretary of State) and must publish reports on their activities. The Secretary of State is also empowered to close down DLOs which underperform. Quite apart from these rules, the drastic fall in council house building has led to redundancies, particularly in inner city authorities.

Thus local government was asked in the Inner City White Paper to make the main contribution to inner city regeneration at a time when its resources were being reduced, and its powers to act on inner city problems exaggerated. The introduction of public participation techniques, especially in planning and in housing improvement, raised the residents' expectations for change, which the local authorities were then unable to satisfy. The partnership arrangements in particular encouraged certain authorities to spend more, and when they did so they were penalized for being 'profligate' and 'spendthrift'. Perhaps, in any case, it was always a pious and unpractical hope to believe that local government alone could achieve the regeneration of the inner cities.

Private sector

This comprises those organizations primarily concerned with making a profit or a return on capital, and includes companies (e.g. in industry, retail, distribution, property development and construction) and financial institutions (e.g. banks and pension funds). In the Inner City White Paper and at dinners and other gatherings of the financial establishment, the Government expressed the hope that the private sector would contribute to inner city regeneration, and the Conservative Government after 1979 stressed the role of private enterprise even more strongly. As the Inner City White paper put it:

> The absence of much spontaneous growth and regeneration is one of the hallmarks of the inner areas. By contrast inner areas have been the scene of intense activity by the public sector, but concentrated very much on housing, redevelopment and, in some instances, on urban road building . . . Local authorities now need . . . to stimulate investment by the private sector, firms and individuals, in industry, commerce and housing. The resources and energies of small and medium sized firms are essential if real progress is to be made and the diversity and vitality, for so long characteristic of inner cities is to be restored . . . The aim must be to encourage changes in the attitudes of industry and financial institutions so that they play their full part (p. 9).

Although prepared to make expressions of good will, the private

Figure 4 Shop fronts. 19th century industrial buildings with small shops on the ground floor and living accommodation above. The empty shop shows the decline of small shops in the inner city and the difficulty of finding suitable new uses.

sector has been generally cautious and sceptical about the new inner city role asked of it by the Government. There appears to be an unbridgeable gap between, on the one hand, the situation in the inner cities, with a decaying physical fabric, demoralized and poorly skilled workforce, complex inter-relationships and fragile economic base, and, on the other hand, the criteria for private investment, particularly long-term investment by financial institutions, of security, growth prospects, attractive environment, simplicity of operation and a firm economic base. The inner cities on this evidence seem to compete miserably with other opportunities for large-scale private investment.

Retailing exemplifies this mismatch between the realities of the inner city and those of the private sector. Recent trends in retailing have been the concentration of trade in the hands of the chain-store groups, larger shops with more efficient floorspace to turnover ratios, and the dominance of road transport (both for delivery of goods to the store and for collection by the customer). The inner city in principle should attract retailers because it offers bigger and more concentrated markets than elsewhere, but in practice it is full of problems for them: too many small, marginally economic shops, low purchasing power and falling population, inconvenient road network, security and pilferage problems, difficulties of site assembly for larger stores. Tesco, whose founder Sir Jack Cohen started as a market-stall trader in the East End, has kept an interest in the inner city as a location for its stores, to the extent of publishing its views on retailing in the inner city, but new retail development has tended to concentrate in the outer areas where site provision is easier, and to close down less profitable inner city stores.

To overcome the disadvantages in the inner city situation, preconditions for private sector intervention have been debated, particularly the removal of bureaucratic controls, the creation of new financial mechanisms, and partnership arrangements between private and public sectors. The burdens of form-filling, industrial development certificates, development land tax, planning controls and other bureaucratic obstacles in the path of the thrusting entrepreneur have been a favourite theme of those representing the private sector. As part of inner city policy, some of these controls have been relaxed, and tax concessions made to industrialists and developers, while the introduction of enterprise zones has been intended to ease the burdens on private enterprise, but the removal of bureaucratic constraints is likely to be more a psychological than a real contribution to the viability of business enterprises.

New financial mechanisms have also been proposed to overcome the speculative nature and low financial return of inner city regeneration, which has made it unattractive to institutional investors. Slough Estates proposed a development bond, with low interest but tax exemptions, which might attract institutional investors with short-term liquidity surpluses, provided there was close regulation of qualifying investments. The government has been reluctant to pursue the idea because of the loss of tax revenue that would be involved, but if it is not introduced, then some other form of investment will be required which may make a heavier burden on the public sector than the lost tax revenue. After an initial slow response, inevitable because of their innate conservatism, some financial institutions have begun to experiment with more adventurous inner city funding proposals, partly prompted by slack demand for investment finance generally. Some banks have begun offering start-up capital to new businesses, even without a proven track record, and both banks and building societies have shown themselves more willing to enter into the inner city housing market.

The fear of further disorders like those of 1980 and 1981 (when premises of financial institutions were a particular target for the rioters), and continued pressure from Government, have, however, encouraged financial institutions to re-invest in the inner areas, seeking to reverse the long-term trend of centralization and withdrawal of investment from the inner areas. In keeping with the Conservative approach of using the private sector to regenerate the inner city, central government revised its co-ordinating machinery to ensure that public spending was directly related to helping private sector projects.

Nevertheless, inner city policy has not yet reversed the trend to decentralization by the private sector. The larger companies continue to close down inefficient, older inner city plants and premises, increasing the strain on the financially vulnerable small-firm sector, upon which much of the inner city economy depends.

Property developers, who reshaped British cities in the 1950s and 1960s, are less interested in new developments since the collapse of the property market in 1973–4 and, more recently, the lifting of restrictions on investment abroad. There is still some interest in office or commercial development, either in expanding central business districts or in new sub-centres of the conurbations, and some interest in refurbishing older office, commercial and industrial buildings, but the days of large-scale town centre development are largely over. Partnership with the local authority is still the usual method of assembling land parcels for any development that is taking place, because of the compulsory purchase powers that the local authority enjoys. Some recent inner city schemes by private house-builders have depended upon this method.

Figure 5 Disinvesting from the inner city. One of many inner city cinemas closed down because of vandalism and lack of customers. Finding alternative uses for redevelopment can be difficult: on this site, a cash-and-carry warehouse has been proposed.

The construction sector, traditionally a large employer of inner city labour, has also suffered from the lack of new development, and especially from the decline in council house building. The Government's Construction Package was a short-lived attempt to introduce some new demand into this depressed sector, but has been followed by drastic cuts in local authority capital programmes. The rehabilitation of residential and other property has benefited small builders, but this type of building work is difficult to cost and run, and therefore risky, and small building firms remain among the most volatile of companies, with high rates of bankruptcy and liquidation. The area concentration of government inner city policies, particularly Partnership Urban Programme and Housing Action Area activity, has not always benefited builders, because it can create a temporary demand which exceeds locally available building capacity and is not sustained.

Voluntary sector

This comprises voluntary organizations dealing with personal social services and environmental matters, to use the definition of the non-governmental Wolfenden Committee Report, *The Future of Voluntary Organizations* 1978. It has been estimated that cities contain one such voluntary organization per thousand population (Wolfenden, p. 35), and they include national organizations like the Citizens Advice Bureaux, Age Concern, Shelter and the Campaign for the Homeless and Rootless (CHAR), umbrella co-ordinating bodies like the Council of Voluntary Services (CVS) and the National Council for Voluntary Organizations (NCVO), and locally based organizations like allotment-holders, residents' associations and groups caring for children, the handicapped and the elderly. It has been suggested that voluntary organizations are more a middle-class than a working-class activity, but the deprived inner areas have a great diversity of such organizations, notably environmental or ecological pressure-groups, play-groups, ethnic minority associations, co-operatives and other employment-creating projects.

The Inner City White Paper emphasized the role of the voluntary organizations and particularly community involvement:

> Involving local people is both a necessary means to the regeneration of the inner areas and an end in its own right. Public authorities need to draw on the ideas of local residents, to discover their priorities and enable them to play a practical part in reviving their areas. Self-help is important and so is community effort. Some things will be better done, or done more

satisfyingly, if they are undertaken by voluntary groups and bodies . . . (p. 8).

Local authorities had already promoted the creation of local organizations, e.g. tenants' associations in council housing estates and residents' associations in housing improvement areas, and the statutory requirements of the *Town and Country Planning Acts* encouraged public involvement in planning matters. The Voluntary Services Unit in the Home Office acts as a link between voluntary organizations and central government. The Conservative Government after 1979 envisaged a growing role for the voluntary sector because of public spending cuts, although the voluntary sector itself was understandably reluctant to take responsibility for existing social services provided under statute.

The voluntary sector in the inner city has often been a radical critic of bureaucratic insensitivity, and particularly of the damaging effects on local communities of property development by both public and private sectors. The Shelter Neighbourhood Action Project (SNAP) begun in 1969 in the Granby area of Liverpool, was a pioneer in articulating community grievances against the juggernaut of local authority housing redevelopment, and thereby provoked the hostility of both councillors and officials. Many other groups began in opposition to proposals for urban motorways, housing redevelopment or speculative office building schemes, and have developed a wider focus for radical political activity. Since the organized squatter movement began in the late 1960s, occupation of vacant land and derelict buildings has been a means of expressing community grievances and acting positively to improve conditions, in a similar way to the long-established and partly institutionalized urban land invasions by the poor of Latin America. Such radical approaches not surprisingly often create uneasy relations with the local authority.

Financially, voluntary organizations in the inner cities, because of the poverty of these areas, depend more upon state aid than voluntary contributions. The voluntary sector absorbed an increasing proportion of Urban Programme funds (a third in Phases 1–4, growing to a half in Phases 5–9), particularly of its revenue rather than capital costs, and some of the most experimental and innovative projects under the Urban Programme were the work of voluntary organizations. Tension between the voluntary organizations and the local authority, through which their funds were usually channelled, was a major criticism of the Urban Programme, the voluntary sector complaining of local government inertia and prejudice, and local government of the voluntary sector's sloppy procedures for financial control and accountability. When the Urban Programme was expanded into the Inner City Programme after 1977, that tension sometimes increased, with the voluntary sector often bidding against local authorities for resources and finding itself with a smaller share, and complaining that it was inadequately represented in the partnership decision-making arrangements. The Inner City Programme became so complex that new umbrella organizations were set up, like Hackney's People in Partnership and Lambeth's Inner City Consultative Group in two London partnership authorities, to disseminate and co-ordinate voluntary sector bids.

With local government seen as too slow and cumbersome, and the private sector deterred by the lack of profitable opportunities, the voluntary sector has been drawn increasingly into economic and environmental regeneration projects. As one of the promotional booklets on the subject has stated:

> During the past decade there has been a growing recognition by community groups, voluntary organizations and community workers that no amount of welfare, social services, improved houses, adventure playgrounds or whatever can substitute for a healthy local economy which allows people to earn a wage adequate to their needs (Pearce and Cassidy, p. 2).

A variety of community enterprises have been started, usually trading organizations, owned and controlled by the residents of an area, with the aim of creating permanent jobs for local people and recycling profits. Ethnic minorities have been active in this field, drawing to some extent upon the experience of black communities in the USA. Direct community action to remove eyesores and generally fight environmental decay is linked to these initiatives, with local enterprise trusts improving vacant sites and community arts groups specializing in painting murals on gable ends and other suitable surfaces. The enterprise trust idea captured the imagination of the Secretary of State for the Environment, Michael Heseltine, in the same way as SNAP in Liverpool captured the imagination of his predecessor, Peter Walker, in the

Figure 6 A lively rural mural on a rendered gable end in the inner city. Community artists and voluntary groups can improve the appearance of the area at little cost.

early 1970s. The Inner Cities Directorate of the Department of the Environment has therefore promoted 'the enterprise trust movement', with projects in Bristol, Park Royal (north London), Leeds, Newcastle, Sheffield and Manchester, and a suggested private sector clearing house for 'corporate social responsibility activities'.

A new hybrid type of voluntary organization is becoming more common, still based on voluntary effort but dependent upon government funds for much of its running costs. There are numerous statutory powers to give grants to voluntary organizations, but the Inner City Programme and the special programmes of the Manpower Services Commission have become the main channel for funds in the inner cities. Some voluntary organizations, for whom finding cheap premises is a perennial problem, have been allowed to use redundant local authority property (like Victorian town halls and libraries) at a subsidized rent, and the local authority can use voluntary organizations to pay workers for a fixed-period project without increasing its permanent establishment. Voluntary organizations are understandably ambivalent about this method of funding, welcoming the extra resources but not the dependency upon local authority support which can be capriciously withdrawn. The Conservative Government after 1979 expressed its support for a continuing voluntary sector role in the inner city, and, although government spending cuts have reduced the grants available for voluntary organizations, grant-aided voluntary effort is likely to remain an established feature of inner city regeneration and to become more institutionalized.

Conclusions

Of the possible sectors or agencies which might contribute to inner city regeneration, central government has been mainly concerned with research, formulating a policy framework and devising the instruments for carrying out that policy. Of the central government institutions only the Department of the Environment, through its responsibility for local government and urban affairs, and the Manpower Services Commission, through its special programmes to create temporary employment, have been significantly involved. Although the White Paper asserted that the complexity of inner city problems required a co-ordinated approach, in practice that has not occurred in central government.

Outside central government, the responsibility for tackling

inner city problems has shifted since the White Paper was published. The Labour Government of 1974–9 considered local government to be 'the natural agency', and in the partnerships and industrial improvement areas devised instruments for local government to use. But central government shrank from the financial commitment, particularly through the rate support grant, that was implied, and the years following the White Paper have seen a decline, not an increase, in the level of local government services in inner cities. The main area of new activity by local government has been in industrial promotion, particularly building small factory units and providing advice to small firms. The disillusionment of the Conservative Government after 1979 with 'profligate' local authorities was shown in its creation of urban development corporations and enterprise zones, intended to accelerate the economic revival of the inner cities, the one by by-passing the local government machinery, and the other by removing bureaucratic restrictions.

Unsurprisingly, private investment has not been generally interested in the challenge of decayed inner areas, in spite of the exhortations of Government, and has lobbied for substantial financial and other incentives as necessary preconditions before it can be expected to contribute to inner city regeneration. The main exceptions have been small businesses specializing in converting premises and in the financial packaging of development proposals, and certain large retailing groups, looking for locations for new stores in an intensely competitive business. New business ventures, although handicapped by high interest rates, have derived some benefit recently from more flexible lending policies in the financial institutions.

With the promise of major contributions by local government or the private sector not being fulfilled, a more important role is emerging for voluntary, non-profit-making, self-help organizations, particularly in improvements to the physical environment, employment creation and ethnic minorities. New styles of organization have come into existence, notably enterprise trusts, and Government sees the voluntary sector as a cheap and democratic solution to inner city problems, with people defining and tackling their local problems with their own resources – an approach usually associated with the ideology of the Liberal Party. But voluntary organizations can only make a limited contribution and rely heavily on Government grants to maintain themselves.

3

Planning and land issues

The identification of an inner city problem or problems presumes a concern with the efficient spatial distribution of resources. Two important elements of inner city policy have therefore been spatial; the apparent overkill of government regional policies, contributing to inner city decay by dispersing people and jobs, and an apparent failure to use the land resources of the inner areas efficiently. Both of these necessarily involve urban and regional planning, because of its concern with the use and development of land. They also contribute to the depressing physical appearance of the inner areas. This chapter examines regional policy, unused land and planning in turn.

Regional policy

For over thirty years after the Barlow Report (1940) on the distribution of Britain's industrial population, the Government had a policy of dispersing industry and employment, in order to assist the depressed regions and curb what Barlow called 'the excessive growth of London' and the other big cities. Regional policy and its relation to national economic performance have been examined elsewhere and are outside the scope of this book, but the main governmental mechanisms for achieving it should be outlined. Economic planning regions were created, each with an Economic Planning Council to advise central government; and the depressed regions in Wales, Scotland, and North and West were given various forms of Assisted Area status. Government grants and allowances were given to encourage industrial development and job creation in Assisted Areas, and the English Industrial Estates Corporation built advance factories in them. Industrial Development Certificates and Office Development Permits were required for new developments over certain floorspace limits, which enabled central government to control employment in the big cities and steer it to the assisted areas. The Location of Offices Bureau was created in 1963 to promote office decentralization, and central government decentralized many of its own offices out of London. After the *New Towns Act* 1946 over thirty new towns were created to accommodate new growth and overspill from the big cities and to regenerate the depressed regions. After the *Town Development Act* 1952 the expanded town programme empowered big cities to negotiate overspill arrangements with town councils outside their boundaries. The Royal Commission on the Constitution (Kilbrandon Report, 1973) advocated the creation of regional assemblies, with powers and responsibilities devolved from Westminster, but this further extension of regional policy was not proceeded with.

In the early 1970s concern began to be expressed that dispersal policy had gone too far. National population was static after more than a century of rapid growth, and the big cities were falling into economic decline because of losses of population and jobs, a situation which dispersal policies had helped create. The structure of the economy was changing, with high unemployment spreading beyond the depressed areas, and with manufacturing industry, always regarded as the dynamic component in regional policy, providing fewer jobs in the economy than before. The Government, far from being able to direct growth through its regional policy, found itself presiding over a major economic recession triggered by the oil crisis of 1973 and exacerbated by the impact of new technologies.

The role of the new and expanded towns in dispersal policy came in for particular criticism. They were accused of having creamed-off the skilled workers and manufacturing jobs from London and other big cities, leaving behind a declining economic and rate base and intractable problems of social deprivation. In their defence, the decline of the inner cities was the result of forces in which dispersal policies were but a minor factor: only 13% of the population leaving London and 7% of the jobs lost in

London between 1945 and 1975 went to new and expanded towns. Much of the employment created in new towns was the result of investment by foreign-based companies who, having decided to locate production in Britain, were unlikely to be attracted to the inner cities because of their poor environment, transport problems and old building stock. Supporters of the new towns movement, prominent among them the Town and Country Planning Association, argued that the new town/inner city relationship should be complementary rather than antagonistic, with the new towns helping to solve problems of housing stress by offering a better life to disadvantaged inner city residents. Nevertheless, while inner city policy was taking shape, the Government acknowledged the end of the period of population and economic growth in 1977 by cutting back new town growth targets and financial allocations, and closing some New Town Development Corporations. The Greater London Council, faced with as many unemployed as all of Scotland and twice as many as Wales, had already effectively reversed its policies of planned dispersal: its New and Expanded Towns Scheme office (which had operated a registry finding jobs for those who wished to leave London) closed, and the London Industrial Centre opened, to promote the retention of industry and employment in the metropolis.

The Inner City White Paper (1977) was muted when it referred to regional policy implications, which it seemed to consider only marginally important. 'Securing a new balance between the inner areas and the rest of the city region in terms of population and jobs' was placed last in the four 'underlying aims' of inner city policy, and the White Paper went on to say:

> A new balance is required between the inner cities and the surrounding region. A deliberate effort is needed to reduce, and possibly in some cases to end, the loss of people and jobs from the cities as a whole and the inner cities in particular . . . There is still a strong need for a continuing regional policy with differentials in industrial incentives for areas with major structural problems . . . but regional policy does not distinguish between the inner and other areas. What is needed now is an intraregional emphasis to policy designed to help inner areas in the Assisted Areas, and in the Non-Assisted Areas. Loca-

> tion of industry policy will be extended to give it this new emphasis . . . The further development of the English new towns has been determined in the light of lower demographic forecasts and of the part they play in assisting the conurbations and their regions at large . . . but over the next seven or eight years the momentum of new town development will be substantially maintained (pp. 7, 12 and 16).

Central government did, however, make changes to the instruments of regional policy to take account of new priorities, and not only by reducing the new towns programme. Industrial Development Certificate (IDC) controls were relaxed and office development permits abandoned altogether. The London and Birmingham partnership areas were given preference, 'after the Assisted Areas and in front of the new and expanding towns, in consideration of IDC applications for mobile projects coming forward from the relevant region' (White Paper, p. 12). In 1979 the Conservative Secretary of State for Industry, Sir Keith Joseph, announced the reduction of grants to industry by a third (£233 million) over the next three years, and adjusted the status of many of the Assisted Areas, downgrading some and upgrading a few.

These changes reflected the Conservative Government's desire to reduce the dependence of industry on government money, but also the need to reduce the incentives dispersing industry away from the South-East and Midlands, although pressure to make inner London an Assisted Area was resisted. Office decentralization policy was in part abandoned when the terms of reference of the Location of Offices Bureau (LOB) were changed to include promoting office employment in inner areas, even in London, and the Conservative Government subsequently abolished LOB altogether. As unemployment and economic decline worsened, the cost effectiveness of regional policy measures in promoting economic revival was increasingly questioned.

Vacant land

The dispersal of people and jobs from the inner cities, partly as a result of regional policy, has left behind redundant sites and buildings. Because of the rapidity with which land has been taken over for urban uses in the 20th century (such uses accounted for 5.4% of the total land area of England and Wales in 1900, 11.5% in 1965, according to Best), any vacant land in urban areas has been criticized as inefficient use of a scarce resource, reducing the agricultural productivity of the nation. A prominent issue in inner city policy is therefore how to find beneficial uses for vacant land – those unsightly sites tinned up with corrugated iron fencing.

The cities have always had unused land within their boundaries, reflecting the unsuitability of some land for use and the inefficiencies of the urban development process, but it was identified as a major problem in the mid-1970s, particularly by the Civic Trust in their study, *Urban Wasteland*, and by Dr Alice Coleman through her work on the *Second Land Utilization Survey*. The Inner City White Paper placed land high (second, after housing) on its list of 'policy changes to assist inner areas':

> In some cities the presence of a great amount of vacant, underused or derelict land is one of the more difficult aspects of the inner city situation. It is bound to affect the morale of those who live in the areas and it may well deter prospective developers who will tend to see it as evidence of the weakness of economic activity in the areas. Steps to improve the attractiveness of inner area sites and to bring land into use must rank among the urgent tasks of the regeneration of the inner cities (p. 27).

The extent of the vacant land problem varies between cities, and it is difficult to generalize, particularly because there is no uniform system of recording land use information. The derelict land returns required by the Department of Environment relate only to land within the official statutory definition of dereliction ('land so damaged by industrial or other development that it is incapable of beneficial use without treatment'), and therefore do not record much inner city vacant land. Burrows (1978) estimated that 6% of all land in the major cities, and a higher proportion in the inner areas, was vacant or derelict (the Glasgow eastern area being the worst with 20% vacant land), and the size of vacant site averaged 0.7 of a hectare in the inner and 2.2 hectares in the outer areas. Birmingham Inner City Partnership found 6% of its inner area vacant in 1980, but only surveyed sites larger than 0.2 of a hectare. The London Borough of Hackney's comprehensive land use survey system in 1978 identified 350 vacant sites (2.4% of the borough's total land area), of which only twenty were larger than an acre (0.4 of a hectare), and the average size was 0.1 of a hectare.

There are various reasons for these high rates of land vacancy. Some land has always been unused because of drainage, ground or other special conditions, but most is land on which buildings have been demolished or the former use abandoned. Some sites are the wrong size or shape for redevelopment to be cost-effective, and combining them with other land to create a viable site may be a time-consuming process, reflecting the complexities of the inner city land market. The rate of redevelopment by both public and private sectors slowed down with the temporary collapse of the property market in 1973–4 and cuts in Government capital programmes, particularly house-building. Rationalization of operations may create redundant land and buildings, notably by nationalized industries, private companies, and education and health authorities. Sometimes an appropriate use for a site cannot be determined because of town map zoning or other planning problems like access or noise.

The use and ownership of land has long been the subject of lively political disagreement, and the debate on inner city vacant land has identified two particular culprits: high land values resulting from the rigidities of the property market, and the public sector land-owners, whose bureaucratic inertia inhibits the development process. Each of them is now examined in some detail because of their importance to inner city redevelopment and regeneration.

Criticism of the property market for setting high land values in inner cities should be seen against a background of virulent public hostility to private property developers, who in the boom of the 1960s were seen to have destroyed established communities to put up ugly office blocks and thereby make 'obscene profits' through the planning system. When the property market temporarily collapsed in 1973–4 and interest rates rose, many speculators were caught in a trap, having paid high prices for sites, particularly on the fringes of central business districts, which they could not now afford to develop, and sometimes could not obtain permission from the local planning authority to build office blocks. When these sites remained vacant, blighting the environment for local residents, their owners were accused of not offering them for sale, or of asking unrealistically high prices, because they hoped one day to turn them into lucrative developments – the so-called 'hope value' of land. A Marxist analysis sees property development in big cities as a method of creating new and artificial surpluses within the capitalist system at the expense of most of their residents; in this analysis the property collapse was one of the periodic crises of capitalism, the adverse effects of which are unloaded on the mass of the people by those who control power.

Extensive land vacancy does not only reflect high 'hope values', but other complexities which distort the operation of an 'open' or 'free' market. The system of valuing land based upon 'comparability' (i.e. actual transactions on comparable sites) may produce a higher value than the less frequently used 'residual' method (which subtracts the cost of site preparation and development from the capitalized income of the probable development), particularly when there may be a limited number of comparable transactions. Public authorities may be prepared to pay higher than the market price for land (subject to the district valuer's validation), which further distorts valuation by comparability, and then find that authority is not forthcoming from central government for the subsequent development. Furthermore, the compensation code for compulsory acquisition by a public authority may value a site quite differently from its value in an actual transaction on the open market, or from its valuation on the balance sheets of bodies, public or private, owning the land, especially since the recent introduction of different procedures to account for the effect of inflation on the valuation of fixed assets.

It seems that land acquisition by the public sector has not adequately taken account of the low demand for inner city sites from the private sector. Most parts of our cities have still only been built on once, the inner areas predominantly in the 19th century, and, where buildings have deteriorated, redevelopment may not be financially attractive, hence the high involvement of the public sector. Historically private development has tended to involve changes to a higher value use (e.g. housing to shopping, warehousing to offices), but in inner areas only a low-value use may be possible, which is obviously unattractive to the private developer. Inner city sites, while they have the advantage of a relatively central location, may present high development costs compared with green field sites, because of the difficulties of site and service preparation. Furthermore, they are unattractive for commercial and industrial developers because of poor environment and difficulties of servicing, and for housing developers because of poor environment and the traditional local authority monopoly in this area. Generally only development or refurbishment for office use is likely to attract the private developer, unless the local authority can offer some partnership arrangement to offset the high land cost.

A particular disadvantage of inner city compared with green field sites may be the condition and capacity of the existing infrastructure, often antiquated. A study of the five underground services (water, sewerage, gas, electricity and telecommunications) prepared for the Department of the Environment found that their current and future condition and capacity, while not a strategic constraint on inner city investment, might have a major effect on individual sites (e.g. the apportionment of onsite and offsite connection costs), with sewerage in the worst condition and needing systematic programmes for maintenance and replacement. The statutory undertakers responsible for these services were understandably reluctant to provide infrastructure in advance of development schemes which might be uncertain or speculative.

The Labour Party has sought to bring land under public control, so that development gains would be retained by the community instead of staying in private hands, and passed the short-lived *Community Land Act* in 1976, its third attempt at land nationalization since the Second World War. This empowered local authorities to acquire land needed for development by either the private or public sector, which would be administered through a Land Acquisition and Management Scheme (based upon block allocations and rolling programmes). It also introduced the concept of current use value as the basis of compensation for land so acquired. Inner city areas were intended to have priority for *Community Land Act* funding, but it had made a relatively small contribution to public land holdings in the inner cities when it was abolished by the Conservatives in 1980.

Since the Conservative Government took power in 1979 the

blame for high levels of vacant land in inner cities has tended to be shifted to the public authorities, who are accused of bureaucratic inertia in their land management. Burrows (1978) found that about half of the vacant inner city land, usually the larger sites, was in public ownership, and sometimes a higher proportion (e.g. Liverpool and Birmingham inner areas with over 75%). Much of this was statutory undertakers' land (particularly British Rail, gas boards and port authorities) made redundant by modernization, decentralization or reorganization, but land where there was no commercial pressure to release it for an alternative development, assuming that an appropriate one could be found. Education, health and water authorities sometimes find themselves in a similar position with 19th century schools, hospitals or treatment plants, respectively, perhaps unsuitable for modern uses. Local councils may find themselves, as the pace of housing development slows, left with the smaller, less convenient sites acquired under slum clearance powers (particularly Part III of the *Housing Act* 1957), and may encounter difficulties in obtaining central government authority to incur the cost of redevelopment.

The new Conservative Government, as well as cutting the capital development programmes of public authorities, urged them to release land not required for their own development, although often the authorities would argue that vacant sites were indeed required for some perhaps ill-defined future development. The Conservative-controlled Greater London Council had already embarked upon a programme of selling off its surplus land holdings by competitive tender. Nationalized industries and statutory undertakers were asked by central government to review their vacant and underused land holdings in partnership areas.

A new experiment was the introduction of land registers in the *Local Government, Planning and Land Act* 1980. Part X of the Act empowered the Secretary of State for the Environment to keep a register (publicly available) of vacant or underused public authority land, and to direct authorities to offer such land for sale if he thought fit. Thirty-three districts, mostly in inner city areas, were designated as areas for which registers would be kept, and a large variety of public bodies were involved (including electricity, gas, water, rail, docks, health, post and local authorities). The registers contained information on the owning body, interest held and details of tenants, site details (area, location, access and services), current or previous use, the authority's reason for retaining the land or steps being taken towards its disposal, and contact name and telephone number of the owning body.

A major examination of the problems of land values and planning in inner areas was carried out by a working party of the Royal Town Planning Institute, which reported in 1979. Among the difficulties of the inner city land market it identified the need for public intervention to improve social and physical infrastructure, low demand because of the exodus of people and jobs, vacant land left over from 19th century industrial and public utility developments which have become redundant, and the effects of uncertainty, blight and extra building costs on private developer confidence. It found that land values may still be high relative to green field sites, for instance, where the local authority has to buy out a commercial or industrial user, with disturbance payments, as part of a redevelopment programme, or where a private owner maintains a high selling price for land on which private redevelopment is not seriously envisaged but ultimate purchase by a public authority is likely. Where there are few recent transactions in land, and those mostly public authority purchases, valuations may be distorted upwards due to 'shifting' or 'floating' values.

Some of the Royal Town Planning Institute (RTPI) working party's recommendations soon became irrelevant with the abandonment of the *Community Land Act* 1976, but the following remain important and have influenced policy and practice:

(a) Eighth Schedule rights should cease to qualify as a basis for valuation if the use formerly established in the site has been discontinued for a period, say of five years. (The Eighth Schedule of the *Town and Country Planning Act* 1971 provides that land keeps a presumptive right to its previous use and scale of building.)

(b) More use should be made of the *Land Compensation Act* 1961, whereby increases in costs of acquiring land due to the existence of a planning scheme can be avoided.

(c) Surveys and consultations undertaken as a basis for statutory plans should place more emphasis on studies of the local land market.

(d) Environmental planning in the inner city should lay particular emphasis on public participation, within an overall framework of community involvement. There should be two inter-related levels of plans for inner areas, giving flexibility through general policies on the one hand, and, on the other hand, certainty through the clear identification of proposals and implementation programmes. In particular, local plan preparation should be integrated with the production of programmes for land, infrastructure, environmental improvements, project appraisals and development briefs, and reviewed periodically with them.

(e) Local and public authorities should review their land holdings to see how these can best contribute to regeneration, keep a register and rolling programme of land management, and local authorities should be prepared to acquire compulsorily land unused by other public authorities. These proposals are similar to the land register provisions in the *Local Government, Planning and Land Act* 1980.

(f) Ownership, price and transaction data for England and Wales (held in the Land Registry) should be open to the public and to researchers, in the same way that the Register of Sasines is available in Scotland.

(g) Government income generated by Development Land Tax (DLT) should be directed back into the development process, and towards inner city activities in particular. (This proposal predated the easing of DLT requirements in the 1981 budget.)

Removing obstacles to the development of vacant sites has been one approach to improving the physical environment of the city. Others have been Operation Cleanup, more use of derelict land grants and projects for temporary or interim uses on vacant sites.

Soon after the inner city partnerships were initiated, the Government announced in 1978 an environmental improvement scheme, Operation Cleanup, making available some £15 million over four years in 75% grants to partnership and programme authorities (additional to the Inner City Programme and separate from the derelict land grant). The scheme was operated by district councils, drawing upon the special programmes of the Manpower Services Commission and sometimes on the efforts of community groups. Operation Cleanup projects included clearing rubbish from vacant sites, grassing and landscaping, cleaning and repainting street furniture, fencing, cleaning the exteriors of prominent buildings and removing unwanted structures. A previous experiment on similar lines had been Operation Eyesore, which was a national scheme. Other attempts to improve the physical appearance of inner cities included new approaches to refuse disposal and street cleansing: large-scale waste reprocessing to provide solid fuel and other by-products, skip sites and bottle banks for public use (following from the statutory responsibilities imposed by the *Civic Amenities Act* 1967), and long-distance transport of bulk waste to fill worked-out quarries (e.g. from Manchester to Bedfordshire by train).

Grants from central government are available for reclamation of derelict land within the definition given above. Inner city local authorities, notably the Greater London Council, have canvassed for this definition to be extended to include natural dereliction, sites contaminated by industrial or other processes (e.g. seepage of chemicals from a neighbouring site), made ground and obsolete structures, and the official definition is now more flexibly interpreted in inner city areas. There has also been pressure for Derelict Land Clearance Areas to be designated, which allow a higher rate of grant to be paid.

Voluntary organizations, often provoked by the blight which an inflexible development process creates, have been active in environmental improvements, by mural painting on exposed gable ends, corrugated iron fencing and other visually prominent surfaces, but most significantly by promoting temporary uses for vacant sites. These uses may give the land-owner little or no income, but can be of great benefit to the community. Temporary occupation licences with the owner's consent usually provide the legal basis, and temporary uses may eventually be displaced by redevelopment or may become permanent themselves. Temporary uses have included the following:

(a) Allotments or leisure plots, with private gardens often in short supply for inner city residents. The Thorpe Report (1969) recommended increased provision of allotments and changes in the law.

(b) City farms, introducing inner city youngsters to farm

activities and country animals.

(c) Informal public gardens, maintained by community effort (since local authorities are often unwilling to take responsibility for layout and maintenance).

(d) Play-schemes (e.g. bicycle scramble-tracks, skate-board parks and adventure playgrounds), important because of the limited opportunities for children's play in inner city areas.

(e) Car parking, to ease on-street parking problems.

Such temporary uses, while valuable to the community and the environment, may be unpopular with land-owners (since they may prejudice ultimate redevelopment), rely heavily upon voluntary effort, and often have problems of finance, ground preparation, maintenance, security and supervision.

Figure 7 Public open space. In the background is the Victorian cast-iron roof of the Covent Garden market building. Demolition materials from the market conversion were used in creating this small park on a corner site.

Problems of finding suitable new uses do not only apply to vacant sites, but also to vacant old buildings, many of which may be in conservation areas or be statutorily protected as buildings of special architectural or historic interest under the *Town and Country Planning Act* 1971. Churches, town halls, libraries, warehouses, electricity generating stations and music halls are a few examples of the types of buildings, often fine creations of 19th century architecture, which are no longer required in the use for which they were originally built, but which require expensive restoration or adaptation to fit them for a new use, even if a suitable one can be found.

Planning

The town and country planning system has an important part to

Figure 8 Public buildings. Library, baths and wash-house in one building, built about 1900 by Camberwell Borough (boiler chimney in the background). These examples of Victorian municipal socialism are now expensive to run and difficult to convert to alternative uses.

play in inner city land and development problems, because of the effects of planning blight, zoning restrictions, plan-making processes, public participation and the development control system.

Planning blight affects both land and properties, where the threat of compulsory acquisition for public development exists. In the past ambitious development programmes for public facilities (e.g. roads, schools, health facilities, open space) have been safeguarded through the development plan system, but the recent decline, of the national economy in general and inner cities in particular, has made their implementation an increasingly remote prospect. Compulsorily acquired properties may stay empty because redevelopment is delayed or not required. Some public authorities have recognized reality by abandoning their development proposals, particularly for urban motorways and school extensions, but often they are reluctant to abandon projects which may have been planned for many years and for which land may already have been expensively acquired. So the blight of land and property continues, affecting its value and making maintenance or improvement pointless to the owner. Even where safeguarding in the development plan has been dropped, the effects of blight may linger on in neglected buildings and environmental eyesores.

Planning blight has been a major contributor to the poor visual environment of inner cities, although the planning system is supposed, among its aims, to safeguard 'amenity' and the aesthetic quality of the built environment. When the inner cities were being discovered by the Sunday newspaper supplements, their depressing appearance made good photographs, especially in grainy black and white. Vacant sites are ugly, whether open or fenced in with corrugated iron, floorboards and other materials, and are often used for fly-tipping and dumping mattresses and domestic rubbish. Derelict and vandalized buildings are fire and safety risks, visual eyesores, refuges for tramps and depress the local property values. The streets are not often swept and are marred by uneven surfaces, and the collection service for household refuse may be infrequent and unreliable. New buildings are rare and the exteriors of older buildings may still have soot and stains left behind by the atmospheric pollution that preceded the clean air legislation. The cars of residents and commuters compete for parking space, with each other, with goods vehicles and with stolen or abandoned vehicles, and there is not enough parking space, on-street or off-street, to go round. Parks and natural vegetation suffer from exhaust fumes, dog-shit, over-use and vandalism.

Responsibility for all these ills is often laid at the door of local authority planners, rather unfairly, since their powers and resources to do much about them are limited. They have the power under Section 65 of the *Town and Country Planning Act* 1971 to require tidying up of waste-land by its owner, but this power is of limited practical value and is rarely used. Until Operation Cleanup and other environmental finance became available under the Inner City Programme, improving the visual environment was a relatively low priority for local authorities.

Zoning restrictions have inhibited the regeneration of the inner cities. These areas have a mixed pattern of planning uses, both of land and buildings, because their development mostly predates modern planning zoning and controls. In the 19th century, before mass transit systems and better personal mobility were introduced, working-class housing was usually within walking distance of the workplace, and this left a legacy of complex land-use patterns, industrial and commercial activities side-by-side with housing, and living accommodation on upper floors above commercial premises. Changes in transportation have made the location of many uses anachronistic: e.g. the concentration of factories and warehouses near docks and canals (when water-borne transport has been largely superseded by rail and road) and terraces of small shops along main roads (where increased traffic and parking restrictions make an unattractive environment for shoppers). Some land uses have become redundant: e.g. coal storage yards for the railways (with steam superseded as a means of locomotion), gasometers superseded by new sources of gas supply, places of entertainment like music halls and cinemas falling victim to changes in public taste.

Town and country planning, which originated as a reaction to the unplanned urban development of the 19th century, has sought to simplify and regulate the land use pattern by zoning primary uses in development plans, and the planning acts provide powers to restrict nonconforming uses. Many nonconforming uses have 'established use' rights (if they have existed on the land continuously since before 1964), but the planning system can deny them expansion opportunities or hamper their activities in other ways. Much of the employment in the inner cities (particularly small-firm employment) is in premises which do not conform with planning zoning (in the London Borough of Hackney, for instance, half of the industry is in areas zoned for non-industrial uses). These uses may be extinguished by redevelopment, or otherwise driven out of business by obstructive planning controls. Recently, however, local planning authorities have been urged to adopt more flexible and permissive attitudes, for instance to allow small industry in residential areas where the adverse environmental effects are minimal. A more permissive attitude toward mixed uses within buildings is also important, especially where large 19th century buildings have to be adapted to modern needs.

As well as planning blight and zoning restrictions, procedural complexities and delays in obtaining planning permission may inhibit inner city regeneration and development. The development control system in local authorities was investigated in the Dobry Report (1975), following widespread criticism of it by developers, particularly house-builders, who attributed to it much of the blame for a shortage of new housing in the early 1970s. The main criticisms have been of delays in processing planning applications, negative attitudes by officials, rigid adherence to policies and standards which may be inappropriate in the inner city situation, and too much attention to trivial detail. Several recent government circulars have sought to improve the situation, and the Conservative Government after 1979 introduced some changes through Circular 22/80 to increase flexibility and responsiveness of the system.

The complexities of planning for development and use of land in inner cities, not to mention the political complications, are such that the inner cities have been called unplannable. Planning applications have to be determined in relation to the development plan, and the system of plan-making has also created problems. The first development plans, prepared after the *Town and Country Planning Act* 1947, laid down zonings of primary land use which have often become irrelevant and indeed an obstacle to inner city regeneration. Since the Planning Advisory Group (PAG) Report of 1965 and the *Town and Country Planning Acts* 1968 and 1971, a new system of statutory plan-making has been introduced, whereby county authorities are responsible for preparing a structure plan to set the strategic context for land use and development, while the district authorities (London boroughs and metropolitan districts for inner city areas) may prepare local plans, of which the law recognizes three different types (district, subject and action area plans).

The new system has been slow to come into operation and has been subject to various criticisms. Structure plans tend to be too generalized and strategic for metropolitan situations, take too long to prepare and date quickly. The Greater London Development Plan, for instance, was only approved by the Secretary of State in 1976, eleven years after the Greater London Council was established with a duty to prepare it. The plan was investigated at a public inquiry which lasted nearly two years, and is now regarded as largely irrelevant to the problems London faces, partly because the processes of inner city decline only became apparent after it was prepared. Because of the slow process of structure plan preparation, local authorities may now (under the *Inner Urban Areas Act* 1978 and the *Local Government, Planning and Land Act* 1980) adopt local plans in advance of the structure plan, although the original system required the structure plan to be approved first.

Local plans are now being prepared, usually of the district plan type, which allocate primary land uses and give detailed site-specific guidance to developers. Several inner London boroughs, in particular, have now approved local plans covering their whole area, and these generally show a more flexible approach to non-conforming uses, particularly industry in residential areas.

Once a plan has been prepared and approved, it may operate for ten to fifteen years in a changing situation, and revision may be a cumbersome process. Also the growth of corporate planning in local government has further complicated plan-making, because, while development plans are supposed to limit themselves to considerations of land use policy, these often cannot be separated from overall decision-making and financial planning in a local authority, especially when it has been cast in the role of a major agent of inner city change. Some authorities, in an effort to promote more positive planning, have shifted emphasis toward the production of non-statutory documents, such as planning briefs for individual sites to encourage development.

Planners have also experimented with joint development initiatives between their authorities and private developers, especially where such partnership arrangements relate to commercial or industrial developments which would not otherwise attract private funding.

The *Town and Country Planning Acts* and Regulations contain detailed statutory requirements for public consultation in the plan-making process, and one of the early local plans prepared in London (the Waterloo District Plan) was referred back to the local authority by the Department of the Environment because its public consultation was considered inadequate. The need for public participation remains a major problem in plan-making. Sometimes the planning system is unable to reconcile conflicting views of priorities, and the technical and legal aspects of plan-making (and indeed of Housing Action Areas and much of local government) may seem irrelevant and incomprehensible to the general public. The Government has tried to simplify the plan-making procedures, particularly the public participation stages, and advised local plans to concentrate on identifying a five-year supply of housing land and appropriate small business developments. Outside the statutory planning system a number of hybrid consultation arrangements have also been tried, particularly involving councillors on a ward basis, to help local authorities respond better to local needs.

From the developer's viewpoint, the complexities of plan-making and development control may be a major hindrance, especially when delay in getting a decision has major cost implications. The planning system in Britain has been accused of being slower or more cumbersome than in other countries, and therefore of inhibiting economic regeneration. Simplified planning procedures were a major demand of the developer's lobby which have been incorporated into the enterprise zone experiments. In particular, the outline and detailed planning permission procedures have been criticized as too inflexible to allow phased redevelopment of large sites, especially where the assembly and release of land for development may itself be a complicated process. This led Taylor Woodrow in their (unsuccessful) proposals for the Surrey Docks site in London to advocate a 'developer's charter', whereby the developer would undertake to complete the project within five years subject to a guarantee of continuity of work and good access.

Conclusions

The apparent failure of the processes for developing and using land in the inner areas, as exemplified by the presence of dereliction and visual eyesores, can be attributed to various causes, as this chapter has sought to show. Vacant land and buildings are usually the unwanted residue left over from major redevelopment programmes of both the public and private sectors, now largely abandoned (at least temporarily), and by the decentralization of people and economic activity to more attractive or efficient locations, now largely achieved. The greed of the private speculative developer, the inefficiency of local government and the inflexibility of the planning system have been variously blamed, but the basic cause is economic decline, reflected in a lack of demand and resources, with which the next chapter is concerned.

4

Economic regeneration

As unemployment and the conditions of the national economy have worsened in Britain during the 1970s, economic regeneration has come to supplant social problems as the dominant concern of inner city policy. Britain and other advanced industrial nations have been undergoing major economic changes. Industrial production has been concentrated in fewer, larger companies, some of them multi-nationals, most of them with a variety of products, processes and facilities. The new corporations have devised new decision-making styles, switching investment and other resources in response to changing world trade conditions and local productivity levels. Technological advances, most recently in micro-electronics and information technology, have led to a contraction of manufacturing employment, the process which has been called de-industrialization, and to a growth of service employment. Increasingly complex production processes and skill requirements have affected adversely small firms and the educationally disadvantaged. This chapter examines the inner city economy, measures to regenerate it and the role of transport and mobility in the inner city.

The inner city economy

The Inner City White Paper (1977) placed 'strengthening the economies of the inner areas and the prospects of their residents' first in the four underlying aims of inner city policy, and went on to say:

> First, because of the number of jobs which have been lost through firms declining or dying, it is vital to preserve the firms and businesses which at present exist in the inner areas. Secondly, indigenous growth needs to be cultivated by facilitating the expansion of local firms through sympathetic planning policies and by making available suitable cheap premises or sites for small businesses. New sites and premises, with good access to communications and with prospects of a trained labour supply, are needed in order to attract suitable manufacturing, service and office firms to settle within the cities. Travel to work arrangements also need to be improved. Both public and private initiatives and capital are required, and there will have to be greater emphasis on training and education (p. 6).

Inner city policy was part of the Government's attempts to improve employment prospects and the state of the national economy at a time of recession. A number of recent research studies, notably by the Centre for Environmental Studies, have shown that the inner city economy and labour market are considerably more complex than the White Paper's general analysis would suggest. It is possible to identify certain of their characteristics.

Loss of employment

Inner cities have lost population and employment since the Second World War. The trend was particularly marked between the 1961 and 1971 censuses, when 400 000 jobs were lost from the cities: Glasgow's population fell by 2.3% and employment by 7.8%; Manchester's by 1.2% and 7.9%, respectively. (The results of the 1981 census will confirm the extent to which the trend has continued.) Some of the jobs lost were extinguished by redevelopment programmes and by the closing or restructuring of firms; others were dispersed to the suburbs, assisted areas, and new and expanded towns: of the jobs lost from London since the War, some 70% disappeared totally, 7% went to new and expanded towns, and the rest were relocated within the South-East region and elsewhere. Also modern capital-intensive business and production methods require fewer employees for a given floorspace or turnover than previously. These factors have created a lower density of employment at and around city centres and a less marked 'gradient' of employment density falling away from the city centre.

Decline of the manufacturing industry

The loss of employment in the inner cities has been particularly marked in the manufacturing sector. The share of manufacturing in total employment has fallen nationally, as a result of the process of 'de-industrialization' experienced by advanced industrial countries in recent years, and particularly in the inner cities. Greater London, for instance, lost 40% of its manufacturing jobs between 1961 and 1975, most markedly in the inner boroughs, while Manchester between 1961 and 1971 lost 3% of its manufacturing jobs each year, three times the rate for the rest of the Greater Manchester conurbation. An important aspect of the change was the complete closure of factories as bigger firms

Figure 9 Canalside industry. Many factories in the 19th century were built alongside canals and waterways, before railways and roads provided better modes of transport. Such factories may now be antiquated and unsuitable for modern production processes.

rationalized their operations between several plants, and plant closures often seem to have followed mergers or changes of ownership. Firms preferred to expand or improve efficiency by leaving the inner cities for modern industrial estates outside the cities with better transport, premises and services; sometimes they disposed of their surplus inner city sites, usually for offices or council housing, and used the proceeds of the sale for new developments and operations elsewhere. A study by Massey and Meegan (published in Evans and Eversley, 1980) considered that the stimulus for industrial restructuring came from various pressures (overcapacity and high costs, to achieve scale advantages or to improve market standing), and that most jobs lost were not relocated, but were totally lost as technological changes by firms reduced their need for labour, particularly skilled labour. The withdrawal of key firms' demand for goods and services as they decentralized or retrenched has had long-term multiplier effects

Figure 10 Small industry. A sweat shop near Brick Lane, East London, in 1972, operating in cheap, cramped premises with low capital costs.

on the inner city economy, causing the decline or death of dependent firms in subsequent years.

Importance of small firms

Small firms have an important role to play in many inner city activities, such as retailing, hotels, catering, building, motor trades and reprocessing of materials. In some inner London boroughs, for instance, small firms account for over 90% of firms and 40% of employment. Definitions of a small firm vary, but characteristics of a typical inner city small firm are: less than fifty employees, owner-managed, operating in old premises with low rents, low levels of capitalization and historical links with other local enterprises; such small firms in the manufacturing sector may also not have an integrated production sequence because other nearby manufacturers serve different stages of the process. This complex network of small-firm interdependency was identified by the American writer on urban society, Jane Jacobs, as a key feature in the economy of cities, but it is vulnerable to various pressures: cyclical down-turns in the economy, cash flow and investment finance difficulties, large-firm rationalization, loss of old premises, customers or supplies from redevelopment and increased bureaucratic demands on management.

Unemployment prone work-force

As the Inner City White Paper said,

> compared with their own conurbations, the inner areas of the big cities suffer from higher unemployment at all stages of the economic cycle. In inner areas generally there has developed a mismatch between the skills of the people and the kinds of jobs available. In some cities such as Glasgow and Liverpool, there is a general lack of demand for labour which affects the whole conurbation but is particularly severe in the inner areas (p. 2).

While certain inner areas have traditionally suffered from high concentrations of unemployment (running at twice the national rate or more), the evidence suggests that inner cities are affected similarly to other parts of the country by economic recession, but that they have a larger pool of 'unemployment prone' workers (such as the young, educationally disadvantaged, ethnic minorities and older workers in declining traditional industries). Finding jobs for school-leavers, particularly those with poor or no educational qualifications, is a national problem, but notably severe in inner areas and among certain ethnic minorities. Older manual workers made redundant by structural changes in industry, may find that their skills cannot be adapted to jobs in newer industries, since industrial change is occurring faster than they can individually adjust to it. Men with large dependent families, as well as having difficulty in finding work, may have little incentive to seek it when state benefit is similar to the take-home pay they would receive if they were working; an aspect of the so-called 'poverty trap'.

These unemployed find themselves 'locked' in the inner areas because of their lack of physical mobility. The increasing separation of home from workplace has affected inner city residents less than others, since they do not benefit from predominantly radial transport networks, and are unlikely to travel far for work because of the costs involved and their dependence on the slower transport modes. Perhaps a more important deterrent to labour mobility is the rigidity of housing markets, a problem stressed by the Lambeth Inner Area Study. Manual workers are less likely to move for a new job than the higher socio-economic groups, partly because of their dependence upon public-rented housing, in which transfers between local authority areas have been rare. Attempts by the Government to promote mobility of labour by measures like the Employment Transfer Scheme (which paid grants for unemployed workers to take jobs beyond daily travelling distance of their homes) have had a very marginal effect, accounting for only a tiny proportion of job changes, and attempts to facilitate council house transfers (e.g. by abolishing length-of-residence qualifications) and to increase the supply of short-term private-rented accommodation have been very limited also.

Poor employment opportunities

Not only are inner city residents prone to unemployment, but they have a poor choice in the jobs that are available. The concept of the dual labour market distinguishes two types of employment: primary employment, characterized by good pay, specific training, continuity, structured internal labour markets and good conditions of work regulated by union–management agreements, and secondary employment, which lacks all these characteristics. The job market for many inner city residents is predominantly of the secondary type: denied access to the primary sector by poor job skills, discrimination and other effects of the cycle of deprivation, they can only get jobs with poor pay, status and conditions, which offer little incentive or opportunity for stable employment or acquiring better job skills. Such low-wage employment concentrates in industries with low skill requirements, highly competitive product markets and low capital-to-labour ratios, like clothing and textiles, laundries, catering and distribution, and in these industries women and ethnic minorities are disproportionately represented. The unstable nature of employment in the secondary sector not only creates bad employee–management relations, but complicates the organization of labour through trade unions to improve pay and working conditions. Some of the problems of the secondary sector were exemplified in the Grunwick dispute of 1976–7, when part of the predominantly Asian and female work-force in a photographic processing plant in north-west London fought long but unsuccessfully for the right to union recognition and better pay and conditions, in an atmosphere of growing political and class strife on the picket-lines and in Parliament.

One of the worst examples of secondary employment is the exploitation of female out-workers. Female economic activity rates are slightly higher in inner cities than in outer parts of conurbations, but the work is often poorly paid. When leaving home to work is difficult, women in low-income households may have to become out-workers, paid low wages at piece-work rates for making up garments, bags and boxes, putting circulars into envelopes and similar tasks.

The unsatisfactory nature of much inner city employment has encouraged a pattern of job-changing and an apparent mismatch of skills between the jobs available and the work-force. Examination of *U/V* ratios (the ratio of registered unemployed to vacancies, which relates supply and demand for labour) shows that, while, for instance, there were as many as 16 unemployed to every vacancy in Merseyside in the early 1970s (and the ratio has increased since), there is generally more demand for labour in inner areas than in the outer parts of conurbations, and this demand is less prone to cyclical down-turns in the economy, but the work offered is low-grade and unattractive.

Another aspect of inner city employment is the 'black' or informal economy, where cash is earned for casual, self-employed or occasionally criminal activity without being declared for purposes of tax or social security. Such tax evasion and social security 'scrounging' are by no means limited to the residents of the inner cities, but are often linked to the low-paid and unstable nature of the employment available.

Effects of planning and redevelopment

Large-scale redevelopment and planning control in inner cities, especially since the Second World War, have affected their economic structure. Commercial and industrial premises have been cleared, and new development often makes only limited (and usually more costly) provision for new shops and businesses displaced. Even where clearance is delayed or stopped, the uncertainty of planning blight has hastened the death of many economically-weak small businesses. In Liverpool, for instance, the city council has acknowledged that 80% of the jobs formerly in its redevelopment areas disappeared completely after clearance, and a survey of Manchester published in 1978 showed that 13% of all plants, employing 10% of the work-force, were affected by compulsory purchase orders. The land and floorspace available for commercial or industrial uses seems to have declined in inner areas, and nonconforming uses have been removed as a result of planning enforcement action.

Remedies for economic decline

While descriptions of the inner city economy by researchers have stressed its complexities, the prescriptions proposed in the Inner City White Paper and elsewhere have been simple, even crudely simple: keep existing jobs and create new jobs (especially in small firms and the manufacturing sector) and provide better premises and training programmes. The agencies involved in this regeneration process – central government, local government, and the private sector – have varied in their contributions.

Direct action by central government in inner city economic regeneration has been achieved particularly by the Manpower Services Commission, established in 1974 (under the *Employment Training Act* 1973) to run the public employment and training services previously provided by the Department of Employment. While its activities and reports have not distinguished a specifically inner city dimension, the Commission's decentralized management has allowed concentration on the areas of greatest need, including those of high ethnic minority unemployment, and the inner areas have become a testing ground for many experimental schemes. In the early years of the Commission temporary employment on socially desirable projects was provided through the Job Creation Programme, and was subsequently enlarged into the Youth Opportunities Programme (YOP) and the Special Temporary Employment Programme (STEP), which nationally had 216 400 and 22 400 entrants respectively in the 1979–80 financial year. YOP in particular has been much used by local authorities, companies and voluntary organizations to finance inner city projects. As the economic recession deepened the Special Programmes Division of the Manpower Services Commission introduced other special employment measures, such as: the Temporary Employment Subsidy (to defer redundancies), Youth Employment Subsidy (to bring more school-leavers into industry), the Job Release Scheme (to allow early retirement and so create job openings), Work Experience on Employers' Premises (to familiarize school-leavers with the realities of work), Community Service (to carry out socially useful projects) and Project-Based Work Experience.

Training in job skills was a major part of central government's new employment initiatives: the theory of the dual labour markets emphasizes training, vocational guidance and better labour market information as the keys to improving the upward mobility of the less skilled to better employment. Industrial training boards were established in the late 1960s for the different industries, as well as the Training Opportunities Scheme (TOPS). Numerous inner city projects were begun to help school-leavers acquire some basic job skills and have included enterprise workshops, training workshops, community industry and project-based work experience.

Figure 11 A training workshop built on a slum clearance site with money from the Inner City Programme, and managed through the Manpower Services Commission special programmes.

Local authorities, concerned at the decline of their local economies, have assumed an increasing role in economic regeneration. About the same time as the Inner City White Paper identified local authorities as 'the natural agencies to tackle inner city problems', the government in Circular 71/77 (*Local Government and the Industrial Strategy*) was urging them to 'give industry priority across the whole range of their functions', and specifically not to impede the economic life of an area by too rigid adherence to old-style planning zonings. Even before the circular, local authorities, especially in the inner cities, had appointed their own officers with responsibility for industrial or economic development, improved their information on local economic trends and government incentives available to industry, started registers of available industrial land, promoted new industrial investment in their areas more actively than before and made arrangements for regular consultation with local business interests. Local authorities had taken the lead in industrial improvement areas before they were given statutory recognition in the

Inner Urban Areas Act 1978 and the Inner City Programme gave particular emphasis to projects for economic regeneration, such as building advance factories.

In theory local authorities could make a major contribution to economic regeneration through the direct creation of jobs, since they are usually among the largest employers in their areas. In practice, local government staffing levels have fallen from the peak levels immediately after the 1974 reorganization, under central government pressure to control spending. Cuts in recurrent expenditure have affected permanent establishments, and cuts in capital expenditure, particularly house-building programmes, have affected the staffing of Direct Labour Organizations. Local authorities have, however, been active to varying degrees in using the Special Programmes of the Manpower Services Commission for environmental projects (like clearing refuse from canals or visual screening of eyesores), and sponsoring training workshops, where the employment created is temporary.

The private sector has remained sceptical about the contribution it might make to inner city economic regeneration, since the inner city, with a weak economy, poor labour force and antiquated physical fabric, was unlikely to compete with other areas for profitable investment. The objective of securing the best return on capital was essentially incompatible with the social objectives of inner city policy. Slough Estates in their assessment of inner city industrial development problems, quoted from the Bible (St. Matthew, Ch. 9):

> No man putteth a piece of new cloth into an old garment, for that which is put in to fill it up taketh from the garment and the rent is made worse. Neither do men put new wine into old bottles else the bottles break and the wine runneth out and the bottles perish but they put new wines into new bottles and both are preserved.

The main exceptions to this unenthusiastic approach were the large food retailing groups, like Associated Dairies, Tesco and the co-operatives, seeking to compensate for low profit margins by increasing their turnover and market share. Since Government policy has tended to discourage out-of-town locations for new superstores, the retailers have shown a willingness to explore inner city locations, particularly docklands and areas with large sites available, for their new stores.

Various approaches have been proposed for overcoming the general caution and scepticism of the private sector toward inner city regeneration:

(a) Less regulated and more mixed employment opportunities. Planning enforcement of zoning conformity, industrial development certificates and restrictions on the form and type of new development may have inhibited business initiative, and more positive and flexible policies towards mixed uses of land and buildings may increase employment opportunities.

(b) Closer working between public and private sectors. Local authorities have increasingly detailed and systematic knowledge (which the private sector can use) of the local economy, politics, land markets and government incentives. Partnership schemes, usually with the local authority contributing land and the developer contributing project management and marketing expertise, can bring new development, and for major developments a development licence or charter has been proposed to overcome the complications of outline and detailed planning permission and phased land acquisition. New consultation arrangements for discussion, mutual education and exploration of opportunities have begun to dispel some of the suspicion and hostility between the two sectors and may even have helped start some useful projects.

(c) Careful identification of projects. The criteria for private capital investment are unlikely to give preferential treatment to inner city projects which might prove unwise in business terms. Unfortunately many inner city investment opportunities remain speculative and the institutional investor requires guarantees and safeguards, perhaps from the local authority or another agency involved in sponsoring the project. Much depends upon the skill and drive of the entrepreneur and upon careful research into potential projects.

(d) Emphasis upon service rather than manufacturing industry. Central and local governments have tended to see a revival of the manufacturing industry as the solution to inner city problems, but the decline in manufacturing employment both nationally and in the inner cities will probably continue, and increased industrial production may not create more jobs. The distribution of goods and services, and its ancillary office administration, may offer more potential for inner city job creation, as goods produced outside the centre have to be brought in to supply the large consumer market in the city (the demand for inner city warehouses near main traffic routes exemplifies this trend). Local planning authorities will have to modify their policies: they have traditionally preferred industrial to warehousing development in the belief that the former created more jobs, but modern warehousing and ancillary administration may require a similar employee to floorspace ratio as manufacturing.

The inner areas' geographical proximity to the central business district (CBD) closely affects their economic well-being. Expanding CBDs can destroy socially desirable residential accommodation and other community facilities, replacing them with more profitable office and business redevelopment, while slumps in the property market have created much of the dereliction in the inner areas. Nevertheless new office and commercial development benefits the construction industry, creates jobs and has a multiplier effect on the local economy. Managed expansion of CBDs, with a flexible approach to planning zonings, and the development of sub-centres to reduce congestion, offer as much prospect of regenerating the inner city economy as attempts to reverse the loss of manufacturing jobs.

Whether office development can help inner city regeneration has been the subject of fierce political disagreement, particularly in London. The demand from the City of London for office floorspace has recently increased, with banking, insurance and other financial operations benefiting from high interest rates, while demand for hotel accommodation has also increased. Disused wharves and other redundant buildings on the South Bank have become prime redevelopment sites, and some five million square feet of additional office floorspace are currently planned by private developers. But inner city policy has given added strength to the protests of community groups who claim that the new office employment created will not benefit inner city residents, and that housing and social facilities for those residents should take priority. The proposals for the Coin Street site, near the South Bank cultural complex, met particularly virulent opposition (see Appendix III). Local authorities have tried to negotiate mixed schemes with developers to include housing and social facilities (the concept of planning gain), and sometimes use legal agreements under Section 52 of the *Town and Country Planning Act* 1971 as the mechanism for ensuring the developer's compliance.

Figure 12 Covent Garden market (east front) during conversion (1979). After the flower and fruit market moved to Vauxhall, the Greater London Council converted the building to a shopping arcade and tourist attraction. In the background are the Royal Opera House and Centre Point (see Appendix III).

Within the service sector a growing activity, tourism, offers particular potential for inner city regeneration. The internationally accepted definition of a tourist is someone who spends at least twenty-four hours away from home for any purpose except such things as boarding education or semi-permanent employment, and therefore includes attendance at international or business conferences and exhibitions by home as well as overseas visitors. Tourism has grown rapidly since the Second World War, although its growth has tended to level out in the 1970s, and business and short visits to towns and cities still offer considerable potential for expansion. Tourism planning attempts to balance the costs and benefits, and to manage tourism for the benefit of the local economy. Inner areas offer proximity to the CBD and often a stock of historic buildings and areas as attractions to tourism, while tourism creates jobs and development, and injects money into the local economy through the multiplier effect. Heritage or conservation projects, including historic buildings, industrial archaeology and artisan crafts, are particularly appropriate for inner areas and can be the means of restoring derelict buildings and areas to a beneficial use, as in the case of Covent Garden (London), Gladstone Pottery Museum (Stoke-on-Trent) and Blackfriars Priory (Newcastle). Port facilities, rivers and canals have the added attraction of water-based activities, as in the case of St. Katherine's Dock (London), Bristol Docks and the Liverpool Maritime Museum. The local authority usually has a leading role in organizing such projects, together with business and voluntary groups, and the English Tourist Board and Historic Buildings Council may give grants.

Another possible area of potential for inner city regeneration is what might be called experimentation with alternative life-styles, including energy conservation, community-based activities and ecological concerns. Although the achievements are essentially small-scale and no articulate lobby has emerged in the inner city context, there are a few interesting projects in this area: Newcastle, for instance, has a city farm, waste reprocessing plant and an advice centre on energy conservation in buildings. An ambitious but unsuccessful proposal was for an Earthlife City on the Surrey Docks site (Southwark, London), which would have been an alternative energy and resource centre, combining a need to conserve energy sources with the manufacture and development of new technology in a 'science park' on the American model.

The contribution of small firms to economic regeneration has been much debated, since the Bolton Committee of Inquiry into Small Firms reported in 1970. The definition of small firm in its terms of reference, broadly 'not more than 200 employees', was larger than that commonly applied in the inner city context, and the committee was concerned with the role of small firms in the national rather than the inner city economy, but its report was important in identifying small businessmen's many problems of management, finance, taxation, form-filling, restrictive trade practices and planning controls. The popular economic philosophy of Eric Schumacher's book *Small Is Beautiful* (1973) contrasted the satisfactions of small-scale enterprise with the apparent spiritual sterility of mass-production methods. Politicians began to say that if every small firm hired one more employee then Britain's unemployment problem would be solved. There were numerous government measures to help: Small Firm Information Centres were set up, Circular 61/72 (on the Bolton Report 1971) exhorted local authorities to moderate the excesses of planning control over non-conforming uses, the Small Firms Employment Subsidy was an incentive for small firms to hire more staff in assisted areas.

The 'incubator' or 'seed-bed' role of the small firm in the inner city has been exaggerated, because while traditionally an inner city location has offered advantages to a new firm, firms specializing in technological innovation are likely to find that other locations offer a better physical and business environment. As Goddard and Thwaites (1980) said of such technologically-based innovative firms, 'to base rejuvenation of the inner city upon these types of firm appears to be highly dubious' (p. 32). Furthermore, present trends in communications and microtechnology are likely to reduce the numbers of low-skilled office jobs (e.g. clerical and typing work) and of certain higher-skilled jobs (like printing and publishing, commonly found in inner-city areas).

A particular problem of small firms is finding suitable premises at a reasonable rent. The complications of letting and managing small industrial or commercial units makes them unattractive to institutional property investors, and, while some local authorities have used Inner City Programme funds to build advance small factories, the main experimental initiatives have come from various types of co-operative venture, subdividing existing premises. There is, however, a growing recognition, prompted by escalating building costs, that existing industrial and commercial buildings are a valuable resource, which can be refurbished to offer cheap, useful floorspace at less cost than new development, especially when suitable sites for new development are difficult and expensive to assemble. A large old warehouse or factory, unsuitable for other use and perhaps intended for demolition, can be subdivided with minimal conversion and modernization costs into small units for letting, with service costs apportioned between tenants and administered through a management company. These conversions require a determined approach by the developer, because of the complications of leases and covenants, of compliance with fire, safety and other regulations, and of marketing and managing them, but several such projects have been successful, particularly in London (e.g. Dryden Street in Covent Garden, Barley Mow in Chiswick, the Clerkenwell Workshop and the Rotherhithe Workshop). The entrepreneurs involved, notably Nicholas Falk of Urbed and Mike Franks of Regeneration Ltd, have formed an articulate lobby arguing that such co-operative ventures could be the key to inner city regeneration.

Critics of such projects have claimed that the tenants are essentially middle-class craft enterprises (e.g. jewellery-making, pottery, arts and design work) of marginal importance to the problem of blue-collar unemployment. Supporters of the concept argue that such jobs offer more growth potential than traditional manufacturing, and that any job created or saved is a gain to the inner city economy.

Other experimental schemes whose aim has been inner city regeneration rather than profit have been attempted, usually as a result of a committed individual's initiative. They include industrial co-ownership schemes, community enterprise trusts and commercial premises associations. The *Industrial Co-Ownership Act* 1976 provided for registration of co-ownership schemes, in which the enterprise is owned and controlled exclusively by those working in it (as distinct from co-operatives, which are largely confined to the retail sector and are consumer-controlled). Local enterprise trusts, incorporated as limited liability companies, sometimes also registered charities, and managed by community representatives for minimal profit, can complement the activities of local authorities and the private sector in improving the environment, putting vacant land to use or helping redundant workers set up their own businesses, and have sometimes used the Manpower Services Commission's special programmes to finance new jobs. The Commercial Premises Association, created by a Soho resident loosely on the model of housing associations, has concerned itself with the problem of the old, small, multi-storey premises common in many inner areas, where a commercial use may remain on the ground floor, but the formerly residential upper floors may be unused. It has been suggested that to finance and promote such ventures the model of the Council for Small Industries in Rural Areas (COSIRA) should be used in urban areas (perhaps called COSURBA).

Transport

Transport, particularly in relation to the CBD, is an important factor in the economic prospects of the inner areas, because mobility and congestion affect the job prospects of their residents and the efficiency of local businesses.

Transport management in the conurbations has been reformed over the last decade with new style transport authorities, plans and financial arrangements. The *Transport Act* 1968 introduced Passenger Transport Authorities in the major cities, following the model of London Transport. In 1975, reflecting the change towards corporate planning in central/local government relations, central government funding for transport was consolidated into a single Transport Supplementary Grant for capital and current expenditure, linked to a Transport Policy and Programme (TPP), a five-year programme of expenditure prepared by each local authority as a basis for central government approval. The new metropolitan county councils were to provide a strategic view of transport in the conurbations and their creation in 1974 coincided with a general public reaction against grandiose urban motorway proposals. The Greater London Council's plans for a motorway box in inner London and a massive restructuring of the primary road network were abandoned in 1973 and following the increases in oil prices metropolitan county councils reviewed their road building programmes. By 1977 the Greater Manchester Council, for instance, had scrapped schemes totalling over £450 million of its original £800 million programme.

These changes seem to have brought little direct benefit to the inner cities, which have suffered instead the adverse effects of changes in the transport system. Large volumes of road traffic, commercial, commuter and other, flow through them. Because the buildings and highway network of inner areas generally predate the motor car, they are faced with major problems of securing modern highway standards, pedestrian–traffic conflict, noise, heavy vehicle vibration, disturbance to the occupiers of buildings near major roads, inadequate vehicular access and servicing, and inadequate parking facilities. Proposals for road widening and new roads have caused extensive blight, which often leaves its damaging effects even after the proposals have been abandoned.

As well as suffering the damaging effects of traffic, inner city residents' opportunities for mobility have declined, and with them their access to job prospects. Public transport has deteriorated in efficiency and increased in cost, both to the consumer and provider, while car ownership levels are lower in inner cities than elsewhere. Rail networks were modernized in four British cities in the 1970s (in London with the Jubilee Line, and in Merseyside, Tyneside and Clydeside), but Manchester effectively abandoned its city centre underground link (the so-called Pic-Vic Line), and major projects in other cities are not planned because of the massive capital costs.

The Inner City White Paper did not offer any major new policies or resources for the transport problems of the inner cities and confined itself to general remarks, particularly on the relationship of transport to economic regeneration and employment:

> Commerce and industry in inner areas need to be serviced by transport conveniently and efficiently and those living in inner areas need to have public transport to get them to work . . . The main practical requirement is likely to be for better and improved local roads and in some cases for better access to the primary road network. The Department of Transport would ask all local authorities, including those in the partnership areas, to identify their proposals for inner areas in their annual Transport Policies and Programmes which provide the basis for the Government's assessment of the provision to be made for roads and transport expenditure . . . Local authorities and bus operators will need to review bus routes and schedules to make sure that they cater as well as possible for actual and potential journeys to work by those living in the inner areas and by those employed there (pp. 32–3).

The future is likely to see palliative rather than radical approaches to transport in the inner cities, and to the environmental problems it creates. Roads and other transport uses account for up to a quarter of inner city land areas, and it should be possible to rearrange that space to improve both the efficiency of the transport network and the environment within which it operates: bus, bicycle or other priority lanes or special heavy goods vehicle routes are examples, and in limited situations conversion of redundant railway land into roads. The traffic management measures adopted in housing improvement areas to reduce its environmental damage can be modified, and applied to industrial and commercial improvement areas to facilitate vehicular servicing. The *Land Compensation Act* 1973 improved the compensation arrangements for those affected by road schemes, the *Control of Pollution Act* 1974 improved noise control and the Leitch Report 1977 advocated more socially sensitive methods of cost benefit appraisal for new trunk road schemes.

While major new capital investment is now unlikely to be embarked upon for many years, more efficient organization may offer some prospect of improved public transport for inner areas, and the Inner City White Paper stressed the relationships of route network, travel costs and reliability of services to job opportunities and therefore economic regeneration prospects. London Transport, for instance, faced with a situation in 1977 when one in six London buses failed to run and only 180 million bus miles were driven when 211 million were scheduled, introduced the Busplan scheme, which aimed to improve service reliability by 'matching scheduled mileage more closely to available operating staff': New passenger services were also introduced on existing railway lines to connect the docklands better with inner London.

Conclusions

The policies of recent Labour and Conservative Governments want the inner areas to contribute as much as possible to the revival of national prosperity through economic regeneration, hence the priority given in inner city spending programmes to projects in this area. As the Conservative Secretary of State for the Environment, Michael Heseltine, said soon after taking office in 1979:

> We cannot have the thriving society we are trying to achieve if

> we have the inner cities decaying at the heart of it. We cannot afford the waste of resources, of people and of land, represented by areas of dereliction and desolation around our city centres . . . Our great cities grew and flourished as a result of success in trade and manufacture: it is important for us to look carefully at the measures necessary for them to flourish again. There must be a place for individual initiative and enterprise to get on the move (Statement on Inner City Policy, October 1979).

Unfortunately, in a static or declining economy the inner areas are unlikely to compete with more favourable locations in attracting investment and creating wealth and prosperity, and in recent years they have suffered the worst effects of structural changes in the British economy: waste of physical and human resources, environmental decay, declining standards of services, increased social and political tension.

Government policies seem to have over-stressed the potential of certain elements in the economic regeneration of inner areas: the incubator role of the small firm, prospects for reversing the decline of manufacturing employment, the stifling effects of bureaucratic restrictions on business, and the contribution that business and management advice services can make. Nevertheless, certain activities resulting from the inner city policy seem to be making a significant contribution: temporary job creation, training programmes and small-unit factory development. Also the inner areas have become laboratories for new ideas and projects; the consequences of which and structural significance to the economy it is still early to measure. The emphasis in the new approach has been upon: (a) more consultation and co-operation, particularly between the public and private sectors; (b) more willingness to adapt methods of organization, finance and management; (c) smaller scales of activity, more self-help and self-employment; (d) more improvization using existing resources and facilities; (e) rehabilitation and conservation rather than renewal; and (f) intermediate technology solutions.

5

Improving the housing stock

Providing adequate housing for the large working populations of the great cities has been a problem since those cities came into existence, and has remained probably the most politically contentious, most studied and most intractable urban problem since long before the emergence of an inner city policy. Housing was top of the list of 'policy changes to assist inner areas' in the annex of the Inner City White Paper (1977), even though in practice economic regeneration has taken the larger share of Inner City Programme resources. This chapter examines the main characteristic of the inner city housing situation, measures for improving housing conditions and the prospects for the future.

The inner city housing situation

Older housing stock and housing stress

About a third of British housing stock was built before 1919, and a higher proportion than that in inner city areas, notwithstanding slum clearance. Such older properties are less likely to have the three basic amenities of bath, hot water and inside toilet, although in the 1960s and 1970s conversions and renovations (both with and without improvement grant aid) have improved the situation. For instance, the proportion of households which had exclusive use of a fixed bath in the various inner city areas

Figure 13 In a northern industrial town, 19th century terraced housing for the working classes on the left, and textile mill on the right. Typical of the industrial revolution towns.

grew from a range of 49–73% in 1961 to 57–87% in 1971. The lower rate of improvement grant approvals since the peak year of 1973 suggests, however, that this improvement is not being maintained.

The inner cities are also areas of housing stress. Following the Milner Holland Report (1965), the Greater London Council devised a housing stress index which brought together various census measures of overcrowding which included: (a) the number of households with more than 1.5 persons per room; (b) the number of sharing households; (c) the number of sharing households with 3 or more persons per room; (d) the number of households with no bath; (e) the number of households without exclusive use of hot and cold water, bath and W.C.; (f) the number of households of 3 or more persons, with more than 1.5 persons per room; (g) the number of sharing households without exclusive use of a stove and sink. The Greater London Development Plan combined these overcrowding measures with areas of housing in poor physical condition to identify 'housing problem areas', mainly in inner London; 1.4 million people lived in these areas in 1966.

Low levels of owner-occupation

Although owner-occupied dwellings now account for more than half of the national housing stock (having grown from 29% of total dwelling stock in England and Wales in 1950 to 53% in 1975), and the building society movement has become a major financial institution, holding half of the gross domestic saving, owner-occupation in the inner cities has remained at a relatively low level. The main reasons for this seem to be the demand for newer, suburban houses and the general reluctance of building societies to lend money on 19th century property, even when in sound structural condition. The larger building societies have been attacked for 'red-lining' inner city areas, i.e. refusing mortgages because of the bad credit worthiness, not of the applicant or the property, but of the neighbourhood where the property is located. Although these societies deny having such policies, there is little doubt that their prudent, conservative approach has limited their lending in inner areas, by offering a lower percentage of the property's valuation than usual, or by refusing mortgages on certain house-types common in those areas (e.g. back-to-back, unimproved, large or short-leasehold properties). While there is as yet no legislation requiring financial institutions to disclose their mortgage policies (unlike the USA), the adverse publicity on 'red-lining' seems to have encouraged a more liberal attitude recently.

Restrictive institutional lending policies have contributed to the process called 'gentrification', whereby working-class households in private-rented, usually converted accommodation, are displaced by more affluent owner-occupiers, usually in professional or managerial occupations. This process has been most marked in parts of inner London, e.g. Chelsea and Hampstead in the 1950s, Camden and Islington in the 1960s, Stockwell and Victoria Park in the 1970s. It has been attacked as the mechanism which drives working-class households into poorer-quality accommodation as the private-rented housing sector shrinks, thus increasing urban deprivation; but it has also been the means of bringing higher-income households into inner city areas, thus contributing to 'social balance', and increasing residents' purchasing power and hence the general prosperity of those areas.

Figure 14 Council housing (Poplar, East London, 1962). A medium-rise estate, mainly family housing. Bin store in foreground, little parking provision and gasometers nearby.

High proportion of public-rented housing

The inner cities have higher than the national average of publicly-owned dwellings, about half of the total dwellings in some local authority areas. Local government has been involved since the 19th century in regulating and providing housing for the large populations of Britain's industrial cities, because working-class housing was unattractive to private investors and developers. Large-scale programmes of local authority slum

Figure 15 Boundary Estate, East London. An early council housing estate built by the London County Council in the 1980s. The photograph, taken in 1906, shows the central circus raised on the rubble of demolished slums, and around it the tenement blocks typical of good working-class housing of the period.

clearance and redevelopment began in the 1930s (although the London County Council's Boundary Estate redevelopment in the East End had been a pioneer in the 1890s), and nearly two million slums were cleared in England and Wales between 1930 and 1977. These programmes reached a peak in the 1960s, with over 60 000 slums being cleared every year between 1961 and 1973, and 200 000 new public-sector dwellings being completed in the peak year of 1968. In 1978, however, only 30 000 slums were cleared and 136 000 new public-sector dwellings completed in the whole United Kingdom. The reasons for this decline were not only economic recession and public spending cuts, but also that suitable redevelopment sites were more difficult to find, public opinion was favouring rehabilitation to redevelopment, and owner-occupation was increasing. Recently additions to council housing stock have come more from the acquisition of existing dwellings than from new construction.

Inner city housing authorities are now the largest residential landlords in their areas, and are faced with the problems of maintaining their stock to adequate standards. Large council estates have been sweepingly criticized for the social problems they seem to create (e.g. teenage crime, glue-sniffing and vandalism), for their design failings (e.g. condensation) and for the economies enforced by housing cost yardsticks. Some large estates have even been demolished without reaching their expected life: the Quarry Hill estate in Leeds, one of the biggest and most spectacular housing experiments of the 1930s was demolished after only forty years because of deterioration in the building fabric. The financial strains of managing a large housing stock have been reflected in successive Conservative Governments' pressure on local authorities to increase council house rents to more 'economic' levels, although this has been resisted by Labour-controlled local authorities.

Concentration of housing stress in the private-rented sector

Although the smallest proportion of the housing stock among the three main tenure types, the private-rented sector is more important in inner cities than elsewhere, and has some of the most intractable problems of housing stress. The sector has declined dramatically in size this century for various reasons, notably statutory rent controls (introduced at the time of the First World War) and the growth of more attractive forms of tenure. In recent years demand for private-rented accommodation has increased from those unable to afford owner-occupation or to meet the requirements for a council tenancy, such as single-person households or large, low-income families from ethnic minorities. Private-rented accommodation is often in poorly converted, older houses, with shared or inadequate basic amenities, and the improvements that may be desirable are not made because they would not generate sufficient additional rental income to justify the expenditure. The activities of a few landlords in the 1950s, who harassed tenants and extracted exorbitant rents, received much adverse publicity and prompted the Milner Holland Report (1965), but generally private landlords, whether companies or individuals, have found the return from letting residential property worse than alternative forms of investment. Therefore, in the period of high inflation in the mid-1970s some property companies began to specialize in so-called 'break-up operations', opting for an immediate capital gain rather than a rental income falling in real value: a tenanted block of flats might be bought at one-third of its vacant-possession market value, and the individual flats then sold to sitting tenants at two-thirds of their market value, with a management arrangement for the common parts and services.

Homelessness and empty houses

The worst housing stress is among those who have no place they can even call their own and the plight of these homeless people was publicized by the television play *Cathy Come Home* in 1968, and by pressure groups like Shelter and the Campaign for the Homeless and Rootless (CHAR). Slum clearance programmes and evictions of private tenants have been major factors increasing the number of homeless, especially in the inner cities, and also recently the migration of young unemployed people to London and other cities in search of work. There are no reliable statistics of total numbers of homeless, but the number of persons in temporary local authority accommodation grew nationally from 13 000 in 1966 to 27 000 in 1971, and these figures do not include those staying in hostels or hospital beds, sleeping rough, squatting or split families. The *Housing (Homeless Persons) Act* 1977 recognized the problem by strengthening the statutory responsibilities of local housing authorities towards the homeless, but has not achieved the success that was hoped for.

Perversely, while homelessness increased, the number of vacant dwellings also increased, from 2.5% of total dwellings nationally in 1951 to 5.3% in 1971. Some vacant houses are awaiting sale from one owner-occupier to another and therefore represent the slow operation of the private house-market, but much of the vacant stock in the inner cities, both publicly and privately owned, is empty for a different reason: because it is awaiting rehabilitation or redevelopment. Homeless people resent the insensitivity and inhumanity of the property development machine and an organized squatting movement began in about

1968 to draw attention to this social and political problem, by occupying empty properties and offering rents to the owners. The situation now seems to be improving, and since 1975 the Housing Emergency Office and some housing associations have begun rehabilitating derelict properties for limited-period occupation (usually less than five years), pending redevelopment or proper renovation.

Rigidities in the housing markets

These prevent easy movement between the main housing types, especially for ethnic minorities. Rex and Moore (1967) in their classic study of race and society in Sparkbrook, Birmingham, considered housing a major problem in racial integration, and constructed a typology of housing classes according to method of access to housing:

(a) Outright owner of whole house.
(b) Owner of mortgaged whole house.
(c) Council tenant.
(d) Tenant of whole house owned by a private landlord.
(e) Owner of house with short-term loans obliged to let rooms.
(f) Tenant of rooms in lodging-house.

Immigrants usually started at the bottom of this class structure.

The Lambeth Inner Area Study also identified rigidities in the different housing markets as preventing less skilled and poorer inner city residents from moving out for new jobs, because they are caught in a 'housing trap', unable to buy a home or to transfer tenancy to a better area:

> . . . at present the low-skill workers of inner London are trapped behind an almost impenetrable cordon. Yet to help them move would meet their own wishes, reduce the mismatch in employment, arrest the social bi-polarization of the inner city and, by easing the pressures, make it possible to improve things for those who remain. We do not believe that further dispersal will impoverish London: a less congested London would be cheaper to run (Department of the Environment, *Inner Area Studies: Summaries of Consultants' Final Reports*, 1977, paragraph 31).

The Lambeth Study proposed policies for balanced dispersal from inner London to help low-income families to move to rented public housing and advocated a national mobility pool made up of council vacancies from all local authorities which could contribute to national economic recovery by improving labour mobility. So far little attention has been given to these proposals and indeed the Greater London Council has largely abandoned its dispersal policies because of its concern with keeping jobs in inner London.

Cumbersome and slow-moving procedures for transferring housing are not confined to the public sector. The slow process of obtaining a mortgage and conveyancing a house, as well as the costs involved, seem to inhibit mobility in the owner-occupied sector, thus slowing the process of 'filtering', through which an increased supply of modern housing is supposed to improve housing conditions generally.

Active housing associations

As the rate of council housebuilding has slowed, housing associations have become more important in inner areas, although they still only controlled 1.3% of the housing stock of England and Wales in 1977. Housing associations are voluntary, non-profit-making organizations which provide, construct, improve and manage dwellings for rent to families or specialist sections of the population (such as old people, single people or the handicapped), sometimes with equity-sharing arrangements. The movement originated in the 19th century, when charitable organizations (like the Peabody Trust and the Society for Improving the Condition of the Labouring Classes) built many blocks of working-class housing in the big cities. After a period of inactivity housing associations were revived by various Acts of Parliament passed between 1964 and 1974, which improved the system of grants and subsidies to housing associations from central government, disbursed through the Housing Corporation and local authorities. Although controls over the management of housing associations and arrangements for their financing have been criticized, they have recently been the most active agency for improving housing conditions in the inner city, particularly rehabilitating older property in Housing Action Areas (HAAs) and other housing stress areas, and experimenting with tenant-controlled co-operative schemes. The Conservative Government after 1979 briefly hoped they would play a major role in redistributing housing from the public to the private sector, but their effectiveness has been limited recently by inflation in construction costs and other severe financial shortages.

Improving inner city housing

Until recently the public sector had a dominant role in inner city housing, increasing its involvement since the problem of rapid industrialization and urbanization emerged in the 19th century. Public housing policy since the Second World War developed four main elements on which the political parties broadly agree: encouraging owner occupation; providing public-rented housing for the 'needy'; protecting private tenants through rent control and security of tenure; and improving the housing stock. In the 1970s the share of housing in national public spending grew from 6% in 1970 to 9% in 1976, and public sector housing policies changed, from redevelopment to rehabilitation, to an area improvement approach and towards more comprehensive and corporate strategies.

Criticism of large-scale slum clearance and redevelopment had begun to emerge in the 1960s, with Needleman's studies showing that rehabilitation could be a more economic alternative. The partial collapse in 1968 of a tower block at Ronan Point (Canning Town, East London) caused a public debate on housing policy which revealed the dislike of high-rise council housing by many of their occupants, the misgivings of housing managers about the new estates, the risks of untested construction methods hastily applied and the change in architects' attitudes (away from the high-rise architecture deriving from Le Corbusier). Also, as the worst slums disappeared, residents began to resist clearance proposals, contending that their homes would be better improved than demolished. The massive redevelopment programme began to falter under the pressure of economic recession: 60 000 dwellings were demolished annually in the 1960s, but by 1978 the number had dropped to 30 000.

House improvement grants, introduced by the *Housing Act* 1949 and modified by subsequent Acts, aided the process of rehabilitation. They were available to landlords and owner-occupiers under certain conditions, as a proportion of the cost of improving dwellings for a thirty-year life, in conformity with a twelve-point standard. By 1977 some three million grants had been approved, with 1973 the peak year (over 360 000 approvals). The system has been criticized because it benefits affluent owner-occupiers more than private tenants, who are often in the worse housing conditions, and because the take-up of grants, which after 1973 declined sharply with the economic recession and rising building costs, has not kept pace with the rate at which the housing stock is deteriorating. The *Housing Act* 1980 modified the grant system in several ways, extending grant eligibility to tenants, extending eligibility for repair grants, and in HAAs removing the rateable value limits for improvement and repairs.

Linked to the rehabilitation approach was a policy of concentrating resources on an area basis. After a number of early experiments with area improvement, notably in Leeds and Birmingham, the *Housing Act* 1969 empowered local authorities to declare General Improvement Areas (GIAs), combining voluntary house improvement with environmental improvement measures. Because GIAs were not seen as alternatives to clearance, many of the worst areas of inner city housing stress were not given the treatment, and this, together with central government concern at the slow rate of GIA declaration and house improvement, led to the *Housing Act* 1974, which empowered local authorities to declare Housing Action Areas (HAAs).

HAAs were to be 'areas of housing stress where bad physical and social conditions interact and where intense activity will immediately follow declaration' (Circular 14/75). Each area scheme was to operate for a limited period (five years, with the option of a two-year extension), and was to involve prompt action by local teams of council officers, and housing associations with regular consultations between residents and the local authority. Local authorities were given additional powers in these areas: to acquire land for the securing of HAA objectives, to give higher improvement grants, to compel better management or improvement of dwellings, to be notified of changes in tenure and to give grants for environmental works. The Act also provided for the declaration of Priority Neighbourhoods, with the more limited role of preventing the housing situation in and around stress areas from deteriorating.

Unfortunately HAAs have been less successful than was hoped. A report on them by the Department of the Environment, not intended for publication, was obtained by the Shelter organization, and their magazine *Roof* leaked it in September 1979. This revealed that in the first thirty-two HAAs declared, only 37% of house improvements programmed had been completed after nearly three years, with the rate of completions particularly low in London. Declarations of HAAs (168 by December 1976) were unevenly distributed geographically, with less in London than its share of stress areas would indicate to be required. The serving of compulsory notices for repair and improvement was also uneven, and some Labour-controlled authorities were using the additional powers in HAAs to municipalize further private-rented housing, a policy which the Department of the Environment tended to resist, especially under the Conservative Government after 1979. Among the reasons for this relative failure of HAAs have been: the problems of improving multi-occupied properties without adequate provision for rehousing the tenants during the construction period, the inability or reluctance of owners to finance improvements even with maximum grants, slow and cumbersome procedures, spending cuts in the housing investment programmes, legal difficulties of short-lease properties, insufficient capacity in the construction industry to undertake such a concentrated programme of work and insufficient use of intermediate grants (intended to allow poorer house-owners to improve to a lower standard than full improvement).

The *Housing Act* 1974 also marked a move towards a more comprehensive approach, combining improvement with 'flexible, co-ordinated and continuous renewal'. Circular 13/75 urged local housing authorities to distinguish between the basic housing objectives of increasing housing stock, improving standards, easing stress and meeting special needs. It also stressed the complexities of the factors affecting housing, which local authorities should respond to: social stress, local attitudes, physical conditions, environmental considerations, consequences of displacement, resources and prevailing trends in the local housing market. The move towards comprehensive housing policies was part of the corporate management approach being pressed on local authorities by central government and was reinforced by the introduction in 1978–9 of new arrangements for public housing finance, the Housing Strategies and Investment Programmes (usually abbreviated to HIPs), intended 'to enable local authorities to present co-ordinated analyses of housing conditions and to formulate coherent policies and programmes of capital spending on public housing'. The new programmes were five-year rolling programmes of proposed capital and revenue expenditure, supplemented by written statements of issues and statistics. The Conservative Government after 1979 increased the freedom of local authorities to determine the cost and quality of new housing, with the Department of the Environment no longer prescribing minimum design standards (the Parker Morris standards), but at the same time cut capital allocations to local authorities drastically in the new block grant system.

The prospects for inner city housing in the 1980s do not appear to be good. After a decade of rehabilitation and area improvement, the rate of house building and improvement seems to be falling behind the rate at which the housing stock is deteriorating, and national economic problems restrict the ability of either the public or private sector to change the situation. While nationally population is not growing and there is a crude housing surplus, in the inner areas various factors, among them the increased numbers of small and single-person households, the 'housing trap' facing poorer households, and increased commuting costs, have sustained pressure on and demand for housing, especially flats and smaller dwellings.

Recent developments in inner city housing have reflected the decline in the public sector role: more active private house-building, encouragement of owner occupation and increased flexibility within the private-rented sector. Each of these is discussed briefly.

Private house building in the inner cities since the Second World War has been minimal because of the scale of council redevelopment. Large house building companies have been reluctant to venture into the inner city, mainly because of the high costs of assembling and preparing sites, and have suggested that the Government will have to subsidize their activities with tax or rate relief before they can be tempted in. Recently, however, private firms have begun to build homes in inner areas for sale, some through joint ventures with the local authority providing land left undeveloped after slum clearance, and the developer building houses for private sale. A scheme was pioneered in Liverpool, where in 1976–7 the Liberal-controlled city council made a big slum clearance site in Anfield available to Wimpey, the largest house builder in the country, who built an estate of two hundred dwellings (semi-detached and terraced housing and one-bedroom flats), believed to be the first housing estate built for owner-occupation in inner Liverpool this century. People in clearance areas and HAAs, in easy-to-let council flats and on the council's housing waiting list had the first chance to buy, and were given financial help with removal and legal costs, while Wimpey arranged mortgages. The new properties sold so quickly and were so popular that the council extended the venture to other inner area sites, and other local authorities also took up the idea.

Owner-occupation in inner areas, historically a low proportion of their total housing tenure, has been rising, as a result of 'gentrification', the sale of public- and private-rented stock, and easier finance for first-time buyers through council and option

Figure 16 Gentrification in progress (marked by builders' skips and 'For Sale' signs). Early 19th century terraced housing, formerly privately rented, passes into owner occupation and is rehabilitated.

mortgages. Recently, however, high interest rates and mortgage shortages seem to have slowed this trend, and concern has been expressed that the slums of the 1980s are being created, as first-time buyers find themselves with no money left after the mortgage payments to maintain or improve their newly-won homes. 'Homesteading' is one attempt to solve the problem: older council properties needing improvement are sold, with preferential prices and mortgage repayment concessions, in return for a commitment by the new owners to improve them by self-help methods. Under the Greater London Council's homesteading scheme, the council sells houses in need of repair and improvement to first-time buyers who have lived or worked in London for 12 of the previous 18 months. In return for a 100% loan for the purchase of the property (on which interest is waived and capital repayments are deferred for up to three years), the homesteader is required to undertake all the work of repair and improvement to the property. The length of the period allowed for carrying out the work and for deferment of mortgage repayments depends on the amount of work required, and nearly a thousand properties were sold under this scheme up to the beginning of 1981.

The *Housing Act* 1980 gave council tenants certain rights to buy and improve their homes. While it is early to assess the effects of this on inner city owner-occupation, it has been suggested that the income levels, stages of family cycle and other characteristics of council tenants will limit the take-up. One approach to increasing owner-occupation was by the Bolton Metropolitan Borough, which built 30 two-bedroom houses and offered them for sale at a fixed selling price or on a 50/50 shared ownership basis with an option to buy the freehold at current market value at a later date. Priority was given to people displaced by clearance, council tenants, waiting-list applicants and first-time buyers. The City of Birmingham operates a system of improvement for sale of its own properties.

The building societies are beginning to show a new attitude to inner city housing, as they find themselves competing more with the banks and other building societies in the private housing finance market. As owner-occupation approaches saturation levels, the inner cities are becoming important areas where owner-occupation can be further stimulated, especially among lower-income households. This requires a revision of 'red-lining' policies and a more flexible attitude to mortgaging older properties. The Abbey National, second largest building society in the country, has led with the new approach: co-operating with local authorities to provide mortgage finance in HAAs and forming its own unregistered housing association (which has bought sites in Tower Hamlets and Southwark, London, on which to build housing for rent and subsequent sale). New mechanisms have also been suggested, such as creating unit trusts and offering part shares in refurbished housing blocks.

With most inner city housing still in the rented sector, both public and private, there have been recent moves to introduce more flexible types of tenure and to improve housing conditions by involving tenants more in managing the properties. The *Housing Act* 1980 introduced short-hold tenancies, whereby a landlord can let housing for a fixed term of one-to-five years, with a guarantee of repossession if he wants; this was an attempt to increase the supply of much needed private-rented accommodation. Housing associations have been active with co-ownership arrangements for blocks of flats, whereby tenants own a share of the property and co-operate in its management. Recently, confronted with intractable problems of managing large housing estates, councils have introduced more consultation and co-operation with their tenants, and tenants' associations in both public and private sectors have become more vocal in pressing for improved conditions.

Conclusions

The phases in housing activity seem to fall more easily into decades than other urban problems. If the 1950s were the era of large-scale movement by ethnic minority immigrants into inner city housing, then the 1960s were the era of large-scale housing redevelopment by public authorities, and the 1970s the era of housing rehabilitation and area improvement. For the 1980s there is little prospect either of dramatic new approaches or of major new investment in inner city housing, whether for redevelopment or rehabilitation. The main trends seem to be towards greater flexibility within housing tenure types, and the decline of new council house building and perhaps of the public-rented sector as a proportion of inner city housing stock.

6

Social provision

Inner city policy originated from a concern with the social problems of deprivation and disadvantage among residents of the inner areas. These areas seem to have a concentration of poor and problem households (such as single parent families, pensioners, jobless single people), a high proportion of economically dependent age groups in their populations and a high dependency on social services and benefits. From analyses of material poverty and inequalities in resource distribution, the concept of deprivation was introduced by social scientists to take account of wider cultural factors, hence the development of indicators of multiple deprivation, while the recognition that these social problems are geographically concentrated in cities led to the use of the term urban deprivation. This chapter examines the ethnic minority aspect of the inner city situation and some of the problems of social provision, education, health and recreation.

Ethnic minorities

The term ethnic or racial minority group has come to be preferred in recent years to other terms like black, coloured or immigrant, because those terms were imprecise or unacceptable to some groups. The census in the past recorded place of birth, so that New Commonwealth (all countries of the Commonwealth except Canada, Australia and New Zealand) or Pakistani origin defined most ethnic minority groups, but this is now a less accurate measure, as the proportion of ethnic minority people born in this country increases. The Government's attempt to introduce a question on ethnic or racial origin in the 1981 census failed: a test census in 1979 experimented with alternative questions in the inner city area of Haringay, north London, but the results showed that such questions were not broadly acceptable to members of the public completing the forms and were unlikely to produce accurate statistics.

The population census has tended to under-enumerate ethnic minorities, particularly because factors like geographical mobility, multi-occupation and extended families are more common among them than among the rest of the population, and create difficulties of accurate counting. According to the 1971 census, two-thirds of the ethnic minorities of England and Wales, but only one-third of the general population, lived in the conurbations, and the ethnic minorities were concentrated in the inner city areas. In 1971 the national average, slightly over 2% of the total population, was considerably exceeded in some conurbations e.g. 6.4% of the population of Greater London was of New Commonwealth origin, in the West Midlands this figure was 5.1% and in West Yorkshire it was 3.2%. Large ethnic minorities include West Indians (two-thirds of them in London), Asians (from India, Pakistan, Bangladesh and East Africa), the Greek and Turkish Cypriots. Most of these immigrants were initially attracted by the 'pull' factor of jobs (because of unskilled and semiskilled labour shortages in the 1950s and 1960s), combined with 'push' factors of economic and political instabilities in their home countries; but recent immigration controls have reduced the numbers of new immigrants. The Office of Population Censuses and Surveys estimates that in 1986 there will be 2.5 to 2.75 million people of New Commonwealth and Pakistani origin in Britain.

Ethnic minorities are an important aspect of the inner city problem, but the White Paper was cautious on the subject, reflecting the central government view that they were the primary concern of the Home Office, not the Department of the Environment. The White Paper devoted three paragraphs out of 103 to the ethnic problem, in which it stated (p. 4):

> The Government intend to ensure that their particular needs are fully taken into account in the planning and implementa-

> tion of policies for the inner areas and in the allocation of resources under the enlarged Urban Programme. However, the attack on the specific problem of racial discrimination and the resultant disadvantages must be primarily through the new anti-discrimination legislation and the work of the Commission for Racial Equality . . . Inner areas problems and racial problems are by no means co-terminous.

Reflecting this attitude, ethnic minorities received relatively little attention in the various inner city research and policy studies, apart from work by the Institute of Race Relations, the Commission for Community Relations and its successor the Commission for Racial Equality, and the research and survey organization Political and Economic Planning (PEP).

Government policy attempts to distinguish racial discrimination from racial disadvantage. The *Race Relations Acts* 1965 and 1968 legislated against racial discrimination, setting up the Race Relations Board to enforce the law and the Community Relations Commission to promote better race relations. The *Race Relations Act* 1976 further strengthened the law and merged the two bodies into the Commission for Racial Equality, which has responsibility for working towards the elimination of racial discrimination, particularly in employment, to promote equality of opportunity and good relations between racial groups, and to review the working of the 1976 Act. The Government sees racial disadvantage differently, as comprising the problems of cultural alienness, low status, material and environmental deprivation, which is shared with disadvantaged whites, but is multiplied and accentuated by racial discrimination.

Identifying the occurrence of racial disadvantage is difficult, not least because it varies between ethnic minorities, but some broad aspects can be outlined. Ethnic minorities tend to be concentrated in areas of older, poor quality, rented housing, both public and private, often shared accommodation, over-crowded and lacking amenities. Ethnic minorities tend to have less well-paid and less desirable jobs, such as street cleansing, garment-making, and on public transport shift work; they also have higher unemployment rates than the rest of the population (the West Indians, for instance, have twice the unemployment rate of the total population). In family life ethnic minorities may be disadvantaged by high ratios of dependents to wage-earners, high proportions of single parent families (notably among West Indians), and divided families (because of immigration restrictions). Ethnic minorities are also disadvantaged in educational qualifications and command of the English language, although the Asian community has a strong commitment to education as the key to self-improvement, which tends to overcome the other disabilities they encounter in the educational system.

Racial disadvantage has proved to be a most intractable problem for central or local government action, and the policy proposals made so far have been noticeably feeble. Local authority housing, education and social services are exhorted to discriminate positively in favour of ethnic minorities in their programmes, to adapt services to give equality of access to them, and to monitor the use of their services by ethnic minorities, but the ethnic groups themselves find such exhortations unconvincing, and the Commission for Racial Equality (the main central government agency concerned with their problems) ineffectual. One of the few successes seems to be English language teaching to adults, through Adult Education Institutes and Industrial Language Training Units, although primary and secondary schools still fail to respond adequately to the language and cultural needs of their pupils (given, for instance, that a tenth of inner London's school-children do not speak English at home). The dominant problem remains, however, the difficulty of ethnic minorities in finding employment.

The most likely stimulus to change is the government's fear of a major eruption of racial violence in inner areas. Harold Wilson, when he launched the Urban Programme in 1968, was partly concerned that the race riots in the USA the previous summer might also occur in Britain; and in the late 1970s, with ethnic minority frustrations increased by economic recession, several disturbances took place which could be interpreted as race riots. In 1976–7 protest at the exploitation of Asian women workers at the Grunwick photo-processing plant in an inner area of north London widened into a dispute over union recognition, with violent demonstrations outside the factory gates. During the general election campaign of 1979 a political meeting of the National Front, provocatively held in Southall, an area of inner London with a large Asian population, led to a demonstration in which Blair Peach, a white teacher and political radical from east

London, was killed. The circumstances of his death provoked a *cause célèbre*, with claims that the police special patrol group had deliberately killed him. In 1980 the police arrest of a black youth at a cafe in the St. Paul's area of inner Bristol led to a riot in which the police had to withdraw from the district and there was looting and damage to property, although the Government nervously claimed that it was not a race riot since the stone-throwers and looters were white as well as black.

The riots in Brixton in April 1981 showed the breakdown of relations between the police and the black community of south London, and were followed by a Home Office inquiry. Insensitive and aggressive local policing methods were criticized at the inquiry, and police training methods modified to include more on community policing. Unemployed black youths, on the streets because they had nowhere else to go, alleged police harassment under the so-called 'sus' law (the *Vagrancy Act* 1824 refers to suspicion of loitering with intent to commit an offence), and the law was changed by the *Criminal Attempts Act* 1981. In spite of these placatory gestures, some ethnic minority groups still urged their supporters not to co-operate with what they considered to be the racist authorities, and the activities of the National Front, transferring the East End anti-semitism of the 1930s to the newer ethnic minorities, contribute to racial tensions in the inner city.

Lord Justice Scarman was appointed by Home Secretary Whitelaw to investigate the causes of the Brixton riots. His report in November 1981 made a number of recommendations to improve relations between police and community, for instance, local statutory liaison committees to make the police more accountable, reform of the police complaints procedure, better and longer police training, more ethnic minority recruitment into the police, and racially prejudiced police behaviour to be a criminal offence. On the wider issues he called the failure of attempts to block inner city decline 'striking', but his remedies only restated central government orthodoxies: more co-ordinated action, and a more direct attack on racial disadvantage, particularly in the three areas of housing, education and employment. While Scarman's appraisal of the policing issues was well received, the constitution of his investigation (a one-man report by a judge rather than by a larger team of mixed professions) limited its scope, and the analysis of socio-economic issues was necessarily limited. His statement, for instance, that institutional racism does not exist in Britain did not reassure the ethnic minority groups.

Perhaps the most notable feature of inner city racial discrimination has been the concentration of ethnic minorities into near-ghettoes, sometimes quaintly called 'distinctive clusters of multiple deprivation'. The 'city ecology' theories of the Chicago school of urban sociologists provide a model for the emergence of this pattern of ethnic segregation: only in the zone of transition (or inner city) can the immigrant find the cheap rented housing and the starting job (in manual or service employment) which he needs. The antagonism of the host society, and the arrival of later immigrants in a 'migration chain', reinforces this geographical segregation, and the ghetto emerges and becomes historically perpetuated after the main period of immigration is over. The usual response of the British Government has been, where possible, to disperse ethnic minorities over the country and within cities (this was done with the Vietnamese 'boat people'), and thereby to absorb them into the host culture. This dispersal policy may, however, increase ethnic minorities' sense of social isolation, reduce their security against racial persecution and inhibit the emergence of ethnic group political and self-help organizations. Indeed, the policy of cultural absorption is itself discriminatory and does not tolerate cultural heterogeneity. Only now is the teaching of ethnic minority history and culture slowly being introduced in schools, and a few councils have begun, experimentally, to allow concentrations of ethnic groups on certain housing estates. For instance, in 1978 the Greater London Council considered setting aside blocks of flats for Bengali use on their housing estates in Spitalfields (where Bengalis had suffered persecution by the National Front in the Brick Lane neighbourhood); although it was suggested that transfers out would be allowed for white tenants who did not like their new neighbours. The Greater London Council retreated from its position by subsequently reaffirming that its housing stock would be organized on a racially segregated basis.

Education

The educational sector developed one of the early 'area'

approaches to urban deprivation; the concept of educational priority areas (EPAs). Concern that the schools should provide equality of opportunity and a compensatory mechanism for disadvantaged children was part of the background to the 1967 Plowden Report, *Children and their Primary Schools.* The education supplementary grant system at that time was already adjusted for demographic characteristics (e.g. school-age population as proportion of total, and population density), and Plowden used certain other criteria to identify EPAs, which were later refined in Circular 11/67; these included occupational characteristics, households receiving state supplements, overcrowding of houses, lack of basic housing amenities, poor attendance at schools, proportions of handicapped pupils, immigrant children, teacher turnover and pupil turnover. Plowden made various recommendations for assisting these areas:

(a) Improve staff to pupil ratios, and give teachers extra pay.
(b) Provide teachers' aides.
(c) Give these areas priority in capital programmes, especially for remodelling schools and for minor works.
(d) Provide extra books and equipment.
(e) Expand nursery education.
(f) Employ 'immobile' teachers available in each area (e.g. qualified married women willing to work but unable to work in other areas).
(g) Establish links between schools and colleges of education.
(h) Establish teachers' centres for in-service training.
(i) Develop social work in conjunction with schools.
(j) Experiment with community schools.
(k) Diversify their social composition.
(l) Monitor progress.
(m) Increase Exchequer grants to local authorities with EPAs.

Most of these recommendations have been put into effect since Plowden reported in 1967, but her area approach has been criticized for not taking sufficient account of class and cultural factors in educational disadvantage, and it has been suggested that helping schools of exceptional difficulty is better than the area approach for helping the disadvantaged. Notwithstanding the Plowden Report, over a decade later the deprived areas still seem to create educational disadvantage as much as ever. Tunley,

Travers and Pratt (1979) found in their detailed study of education in the London Borough of Newham, that it was the schools in deprived areas which suffered most when educational spending was cut.

The Inner City White Paper (1977) proposed certain policy changes in education to assist inner areas (paragraphs 23–6 of the Annex) which recall those made in the Plowden Report ten years before: remodelling and renewal of existing schools, fuller involvement of schools in the life of the community, improving teaching standards in schools with a higher than average proportion of disadvantaged children, a better under-fives service, better youth and community welfare services. Education authorities were included in the allocation of Inner City Programme funds, which were used particularly to remodel schools for which finances would not otherwise have been available. Many schools are in 19th century buildings (constructed following the *Education Act* 1870 which introduced universal compulsory schooling) in slum areas, with little provision for outdoor play, and the funds have been used to enlarge the curtilages of schools and make better play facilities.

The emergence of an inner city policy coincided with demographic changes leading to a decline in school enrollments, and this decline has been particularly drastic in inner city areas. As pupil numbers fall, the educational system favours larger schools, closure and merging of schools become necessary and have to be negotiated with parents, teachers and unions, who may want to protect their convenience and the status quo. Furthermore, the development plans prepared in a time of growth reserved large areas of inner city land for educational purposes. Much of this has not been taken up and is now surplus to educational requirements, adding to the inner city's problems of redundant land and buildings.

Inner city policy has also coincided with growing criticism of the school system for failing to supply an education (or even adequate standards of literacy) appropriate to the jobs that may be available. Rising unemployment among school-leavers has eroded their confidence that schooling helps them get a job (especially among West Indians, who have particularly high levels of school-leaver unemployment), and therefore truancy and poor academic performance are perpetuated. Recent reports of the Schools Inspectorate have emphasized the difficulty of maintaining staff and student morale. They also emphasized the need for a sense of social relevance in schools which are located in the decaying environment and economy of the inner areas. Post-school education, particularly through Colleges of Further Education, has provided some opportunity to correct these disadvantages, and the special programmes of the Manpower Services Commission have concentrated recently upon training workshops and other measures to provide relevant job skills to young unemployed in the inner cities.

Recreation

After the three waves of industrialization, railway-building and suburbanization which have swept over Britain in the past two centuries, the need to provide for a fourth wave, increased leisure time for the mass of the population, was much debated in the 1960s. Inner cities, however, seem to have benefited little from increased general leisure provision, and leisure and recreation receive little mention in the White Paper, apart from the environment policy area, where local authorities are encouraged to 'give priority to the inner areas in the provision of small-scale sports and recreation facilities, especially for young people, and places for children to play' (paragraph 21 of the Annex). This seems to indicate that the government sees recreation as only marginally relevant to the main objectives of inner city policy, but also reflects the low effective demand from inner city residents because of their demographic and social composition. Demand for active recreation comes more from the higher income, higher social class and more mobile households, which are a small proportion of inner city residents. Demand for active recreation also declines with age, and the inner cities have a higher proportion of older people than other areas.

Although expressed or effective demand may be lower, there is nevertheless a great need for leisure and recreation facilities in the inner city. The unemployed and retired may find time heavy on their hands, but do not have the money or mobility to enjoy their enforced leisure. Unemployed school-leavers may be on the streets because they have nowhere to go and nothing to do with their time: lack of recreational facilities and organized recreation programmes was found to be a major cause of the 1967 race riots in the cities of the USA. Children may also lack adequate play facilities at school or at home. With such frustrations, it is not surprising that crimes against persons and property are more common in inner areas, or that glue-sniffing and petty theft are a means of escapist excitement to the young in those areas.

The new local authorities created in the 1974 reorganization recognized the importance of leisure and recreation, with new departments and directorates taking on wider responsibilities than the former parks or amenities departments. But finance in this area has been severely inhibited by the lack of central government support, and has to be found from the hard-pressed locally determined sector. The Sports Council offers capital grants for sports facilities in areas of 'special need' (defined in relation to recognized national standards, population density, unemployment, low socio-economic groupings, high proportion of the population in the 15–25 age group and a high degree of recreational deprivation); grants are available for 50% of approved cost, to a maximum of £50 000 per grant. Private finan-

Figure 17 A public park being created on a slum clearance site in a densely-populated inner area. The cost can be high because of the need to clear the site, divert underground services, and import topsoil and landscaping.

cial initiatives have been limited because of the difficulty of generating sufficient income to cover running costs and debt charges, although some experiments have been made where there is a high potential tourist demand.

The most visible recreational expenditure in the 1970s was the building of large sports centres, but these often do not benefit inner city residents, even when located in inner areas and even when charges are set below the commercial rate. It has been found that, the larger a facility, the less it serves its immediate local population. For instance, the Michael Sobell Sports Centre in Islington, which opened in 1973, has the largest indoor arena in Britain, a practice hall, projectile hall, multi-purpose hall, weight-training room, squash courts, saunas, ice-skating rink, catering and meeting rooms; but it has not benefited the local disadvantaged residents, since very few unskilled or semi-skilled workers go there, two-thirds of the users come from car-owning households and only 4% of spectators live in Islington. Squash is the dominant activity of the members and 60% of its participants are drawn from social classes I and II. Another example is the

Figure 18 An overgrown Victorian cemetery (Abney Park, see Appendix III) becomes a semi-wilderness area for the public, under local authority management.

Moss Side Leisure Centre, one of three such centres built in Manchester in the 1970s, which has swimming pools, sports hall and the usual other facilities. Despite low entry charges and a quarter of a million people within a four kilometre radius, the centre is little used, even the squash courts, and a billiard-room was closed because of thefts and vandalism. It is in a typical area of inner city deprivation with some notorious large council estates nearby and is under-used apparently because local residents feel it is irrelevant to their needs, while other potential users are deterred by the notoriety of the area.

The provision of parks and public open space (POS) in inner areas that have always lacked them poses particular problems. Some inner areas are well provided with parks, usually either commons protected from enclosure, or the gifts of wealthy public benefactors, but some areas have an acute shortage, particularly of local parks. The *Open Space Act* 1906 and other legislation gives local government the appropriate statutory powers, and development plans usually now attempt to allocate POS land in a hierarchy of regional parks, urban parks and local parks. But some of this planned POS has remained unimplemented for decades, particularly because of financial constraints, both on capital development and maintenance costs.

An opportunist approach by community groups can do much to rectify deficiencies in inner city recreation provision. Vacant buildings have been adapted as community, tenants' or cultural centres, and vacant sites can be taken over as temporary parks, playgrounds, allotments or urban farms. Community groups can work with the local authority to provide cheaper and more effective management of small local parks than the authority itself could provide. Adventure playgrounds have been much advocated because they can remedy the lack of playgrounds while using waste land and materials easily available in inner areas. A voluntary group, the National Playbus Association, which started in Liverpool in the late 1960s, has adapted over a hundred redundant buses, mostly in inner city areas, as mobile play centres for a multitude of activities (toddler groups, adult education, literacy schemes, toy libraries, theatre projects, craft workshops, craft latch-key clubs).

Gardening is one of the main leisure activities nationally, but often inner city residents lack the opportunity to cultivate their own gardens. Post-war council housing was criticized for providing little private open space for the tenants, and recent developments have paid particular attention to supplying gardens, however small, to family dwellings. Allotments provide an alternative to private gardens. They played an important part in home food production during the Second World War, and after a decline in popularity are now being actively promoted as a means of bringing derelict land into beneficial use. Statutory powers for local authority allotments exist under the various *Allotments Acts* 1908–50, and the Thorpe Report into Allotments 1969 (which preferred the term 'leisure plots' to describe them) recommended devolution of management to allotment associations. Unfortunately progress has been sometimes slow in bringing land into allotment use, because of difficulties with owners' permission, organizing and financing suitable associations, preparing the ground and site security.

For all the emphasis on public leisure provision outside the home, it is as well to remember that most leisure time is still spent at home and the most popular leisure pursuit is watching the television.

Health and social services

Health provision exemplifies the lack of a unified approach to inner city problems by central government. The policy of the Department of Health and Social Security is to redistribute resources to the historically under-provided regions, particularly the north, through the mechanism of its Resources Allocation Working Party (RAWP). This redistribution can conflict with the objectives of inner city policy, for instance, where the deprived inner areas of more prosperous regions are affected.

It is difficult to measure the need for health care or to compare standards of provision, but regional variations can be identified. For instance, if the number of occupied beds per thousand population is used as a measure of standards, the average for England in 1972 was 7.4, but the four Metropolitan Regional Hospital Boards averaged 8.25, and Birmingham 6.6, inequalities which the RAWP is attempting to redress.

Health provision received only passing mention in the Inner Area Studies, and in the White Paper appears only in the Annex

Figure 19 A redundant inner city hospital, built in the 19th century, unsuitable for modern hospital practice, and with a declining catchment population. The site is available for alternative use, but the costs of demolition and redevelopment are high.

on policy changes, where it is placed eighth out of nine policy areas identified. The statement is luke-warm about inner city objectives (p. 31):

> Many inner areas are for historical reasons relatively well supplied with hospitals compared with some other areas; very generally there is disparity of provision between the south of England and the north. The new formula devised by the Resources Allocation Working Party of the Department of Health and Social Security for distributing resources will therefore tend to set targets for a greater share of resources to northern regions in England, and within some regions to areas outside the conurbations.

This attitude has also been reflected in the relative lack of research on the health aspects of inner areas.

The inner cities have a large number of hospitals, mostly built in the Victorian period when city populations were at their height, and the geographical distribution of National Health Service (NHS) capital assets has changed little since its creation in 1948. London in particular has a number of large teaching hospitals, and their bed specialties have reflected the hospitals' needs as national 'centres of medical excellence' rather than the changing health needs of their declining local catchment populations: over-provided with surgical, acute and maternity beds, under-provided with general medical beds and geriatric services. The capital development programme has tended to locate new hospitals in the suburbs, following the general out-movement of population: St. George's Hospital moved from Hyde Park Corner to a new building at Tooting, and Charing Cross Hospital to a new building at Fulham. Declining catchment population, administrative reorganization and the capital development programme have all led to the amalgamation and closure of hospitals, and left older hospitals surplus to requirements, e.g. multi-storey buildings, some of them former work-houses from the early 19th century, unsuitable for modern requirements, expensive and inefficient to run, on cramped sites, but still often robust structures.

Local political accountability for these resource allocation decisions in the NHS is lacking, because the members of health authorities are appointed by central government, not elected, while the community health councils, its concession to democracy, advise but do not decide. The administrative structure of the NHS does not help identify an inner city dimension in health care: for instance, Greater London is divided between four metropolitan regional health authorities. The battle for resources takes place within that administrative structure and in the 'corridors of power' at the Department of Health and Social Security rather than in open political debate, and the outcome only becomes apparent as district health authorities struggle to function within ever tighter financial constraints. The Conservative Government's emphasis on increasing the share of private medicine in the nation's health care has tended to reduce the levels of service in deprived inner areas most. Vehement local opposition was expressed to the closure of some hospitals and medical schools, particularly where there were strong community links, even to the extent of staff and patients being forcibly evicted from wards due for closure, but the NHS decision-making machinery has proved unresponsive to such demands.

Because of the relatively good provision of hospitals and their out-patient services in the inner cities, other aspects of health care have received less attention, e.g. general practice, health visiting, co-ordination of health and social services. With the need to reduce the costs of the NHS and the high proportion of old, sick, poor and disadvantaged people in inner city communities, more emphasis is being placed upon community health care, for instance, by providing geriatric day centres to reduce occupancy of expensive hospital beds by geriatric patients and to maintain the independence of their lives. The White Paper recognized this need:

> Health authorities are well aware of the inter-relationship between social conditions and health. They are seeking to develop a balanced pattern of provision which takes account of health needs as a whole and is planned in consultation with the corresponding local authorities. There should be further steps towards improvements in local co-operation, both between health and social services, and within the health service itself. The recruitment and distribution of district nurses, health visitors and midwives as well as doctors, will all be considered, as will the provision of health centres from which they can work as teams (Paragraph 32 of the Annex).

A proportion of the Inner City Programme funds has been allocated to health authorities in Partnership and Programme areas, and the White Paper stated that 'this will help the hospital and community health services in inner city areas to play the wider social role required of them and will reinforce their links with other services' (paragraph 30 of the Annex). Unfortunately the limited funds provided in this way have not offset the drastic reduction and redistribution of main programme resources, and Inner City Programme funds have tended not to be used as the Government intended – to improve co-ordination and community health provision – but more to alleviate the past under-financing of basic services.

7

Four governmental experiments

Inner city partnerships

The main new initiative announced in the Inner City White Paper (1977) was the creation of partnership arrangements between central and local government for certain cities with particularly severe problems. The criteria for selection were discussed in the White Paper (pp. 16–9), and the Government offered partnership first to five areas: Liverpool, Birmingham, Manchester/Salford, Lambeth and London Docklands. Subsequently, after other authorities had submitted proposals to be included, a further two partnerships were created, in Hackney/Islington and Newcastle/Gateshead. The geographical areas within which these partnerships would operate were sometimes all, sometimes part, of a local authority's area and sometimes were shared between two adjacent districts, and, in the case of London Docklands, included parts of several London Boroughs, co-ordinated through the Docklands Joint Committee. The three guiding ideas behind the partnerships were to concentrate limited resources in some of the worst problem areas, to co-ordinate action for dealing with the complex and inter-related problems faced by those areas and to tailor policies and action to local needs.

As to the participants in these new arrangements, the White Paper stated that 'the intention is to bring together the local authorities – at district and county level (London Boroughs and the Greater London Council) – and central government, through departments and agencies, e.g. Manpower Services Commission, Health Authorities' (p. 18). In the USA such arrangements, limited to public authorities with no private or voluntary sector involvement, would probably be unthinkable, and indeed some American observers have criticized the British inner city partnerships as narrowly conceived and unlikely to succeed. The White Paper does, however, say that 'local communities will need to be involved in the planning and execution of the programmes', and some partnerships have gone to considerable lengths to consult the public and local interest groups. The Department of the Environment and the Manpower Services Commission have been active in partnerships, but other central government bodies, like statutory undertakers and the police, have been relatively little involved.

The machinery for guiding partnerships was established during 1977 and 1978. Each partnership was headed by a Partnership Committee, chaired by a Department of the Environment minister and attended by representatives of the other elected or appointed authorities, meeting several times a year, and with a co-ordinating rather than executive role. To service the Partnership Committee and carry forward the work of partnership, an Officer Steering Group was created for each partnership, comprising senior officials of the participating authorities and meeting at about monthly intervals. Usually a small team was also created, with some specially appointed staff and some seconded from the participating authorities, 'to analyse inner area needs, to draw up the programme and to oversee its implementation' (White Paper on Inner Cities, 1977, p. 18). Joint working groups of officials from the departments and authorities most concerned were also established to examine topics of particular importance (e.g. economic regeneration, vacant/derelict land and buildings, environmental improvement).

Financial support for the partnerships came mainly from the expanded Urban Programme, supplemented by short-term programmes like the Construction Package and Operation Cleanup, and often combined with resources from the Special Programmes of the Manpower Services Commission to provide resources for the inner cities in general. The Urban Programme was expanded from £30 million in 1977/78 to £125 million in

1979/80 (at 1977/78 out-turn prices), and the partnerships were allocated about £66 million of this, 75% coming from central government as an Exchequer grant and 25% from the other partnership authorities' own finances. The Department of the Environment retained approval of Urban Programme projects and therefore ultimate financial control, and resources could be used as either capital or revenue (although capital schemes tended to predominate). The Partnership Urban Programme (PUP) represented only a small addition to the budgets of the participating authorities: for instance, the Hackney/Islington partnership in one financial year was allocated £9 million from the PUP, while the combined budgets of public authorities in that partnership area in that year were over £500 million. The PUP was therefore intended to supplement main programmes, fill gaps, support experimental and innovative projects, and support projects in the voluntary sector. Much emphasis was placed on 'bending main programmes', given the limited PUP resources.

The partnership arrangements can be seen as a means for the Department of the Environment to promote corporate planning and management in local authorities, and to increase its control over local government. Thus the same style of financial programming was used in the partnerships as had been developed in housing, transport and other areas of local government activity which had been instigated by the Department of the Environment. Partnerships organized their resources in three-year Inner Area Programmes which were reviewed and rolled forward annually, to provide a co-ordinating and comprehensive approach to spending, not only PUP resources, but also main programme resources. The Department of the Environment also required district authorities in their partnerships, where they had not already done so, to re-organize their activities into 'programme areas' (e.g. economic regeneration, environment and transport), with defined policy objectives and regular financial and policy reviews, and also to strengthen their central policy research functions.

Partnership resources were allocated in varying proportions between the participating authorities, and projects for funding were selected from bids put forward by them and by the voluntary sector. Central government, the main financial contributor, required a strong emphasis on projects of economic regeneration,

Figure 20 Workshops for small firms, built by the local authority with partnership funds on the site of a tenement block in an industrial area. There is plenty of demand for such units.

because of the national concern about unemployment and the state of the economy. An increasing proportion of PUP resources, sometimes over half, was allocated to this programme area (e.g. for factory-building, site assembly for commercial/industrial development, improved servicing and access for firms, training and special employment schemes), compared with the other programme areas like environment, leisure and recreation, social and community services. Most partnerships have concentrated particularly on building small factory units (up to about 5000 square feet), which are much in demand but have traditionally been neglected by private institutions as a form of investment because of their alleged low return on capital and management difficulties. Other partnership projects have included environmental works and landscaping, traffic management, replacement of street furniture, provision and upgrading of open space and recreational facilities, improved educational, youth and community facilities, literacy and numeracy programmes, day nurseries and nursery classes, day care for the elderly, home visiting and community arts.

Figure 21 A sports centre, built by the local authority with partnership funds, on a slum clearance site intended for public open space. The centre provides a sports hall, squash courts, etc., and is managed for the benefit of the local schools and community.

The period within which the partnership was intended to operate was not defined precisely in the Inner City White Paper (which only referred to 'the next few years'), but was envisaged to be at least ten years. Within two years of the partnership scheme being announced, the national Government changed, but agreement between political parties over the need for inner city regeneration ensured the survival of the partnership arrangements. The new Conservative Government did, however, criticize them for over-bureaucratic procedures and for the lack of involvement by the voluntary sector. The local authorities in the partnership areas are, however, predominantly Labour-controlled, and as political pressure grew to redistribute resources to Conservative-controlled areas, and to penalize 'spend-thrift' local authorities, the finances of partnership authorities and other inner city authorities have been cut, sometimes by amounts greater than the levels of the PUP contribution. For instance, when in the autumn of 1980 certain local authorities with allegedly the worst records of over-spending were selected for punishment by cuts in their financial support from central government, they were almost all inner city authorities and several were partnership authorities, who not only lost income from their Rate Support Grant but also from their PUP resources.

In praise of partnerships, it can be said that they represent a Government commitment which has produced some visible results on the ground, such as environmental improvements and advance factories. They have also allowed some interesting experiments, particularly by community action, to be attempted which might not otherwise have happened, and to bring some long-derelict sites into beneficial use. Among the different agencies involved in the inner city, particularly local authorities, they have led to some changed thinking, more co-ordinated effort and less suspicion; also they have improved local authorities' consultation arrangements and relations with the public and local interest groups.

In criticism of partnerships, it can be said that they have thrown up a bureaucratic machinery additional to those which already exist, with cumbersome processes for disseminating information and approving projects (although this in part reflects the practical difficulties of involving many public and private agencies in their work). The co-ordination of effort which the White paper expected them to achieve has not been very apparent, especially at central government level, where there seems to have been little commitment other than from the Department of the Environment and the Manpower Services Commission. The restriction of the partnerships to public authority representatives has limited the involvement of the private sector, particularly voluntary agencies, and has therefore limited the effectiveness of the partnership experiment. Also the 'worst first' approach which the partnerships reflect has not encouraged interest by private financial institutions (although a depressed construction industry has been grateful for the additional contracts which partnership money has created). The financial resources of the PUP were always very small in the context of overall Government spending; and programming and management difficulties have led to substantial under-spending in some cases. The bending of main programmes that the White Paper hoped for has not materialized, especially with recent public spending cuts, so that the partnerships' contribution to inner city regeneration is likely to remain marginal. For instance, at one time the Liverpool Inner

City Partnership's annual allocation of funds was less than the total unemployment benefit paid out in the city in one week.

Beside the seven partnerships, the Inner City White Paper led to a second tier of inner city authorities (the so-called 'programme authorities') which received assistance because they merited special attention but not full-scale partnership treatment. Fifteen such authorities were selected: North and South Tyneside, Sunderland, Middlesbrough, Bolton, Oldham, Wirral, Bradford, Hull, Leeds, Sheffield, Wolverhampton, Leicester, Nottingham and Hammersmith. They were allocated Urban Programme money (starting with a total of £25 million in 1979/80 and averaging £1–2 million per authority per annum). Programme authorities did not have the machinery of partnership committees, or direct involvement by ministers and government departments, but had to prepare their own Inner Area Programmes, showing evidence of a comprehensive approach: some have been active and innovative in tackling their inner area problems.

Industrial improvement areas and the *Inner Urban Act* 1978

The industrial decline of the inner cities has been partly due to congestion and the physical difficulties of operating in them. Their industrial and commercial buildings, dating mainly from the 19th century, while often solidly constructed, may not comply with modern health, safety and fire regulations, nor adapt easily to modern processes. These buildings may be multi-storey on cramped sites in narrow streets so that access for goods vehicles is poor, and parking for employees and visitors inadequate (especially with recent traffic measures to curb the use of the private motor car). Other problems include the juxtaposition of conflicting land uses (perhaps unneighbourly but with established use rights because they predate planning controls), and historical anomalies in the division, ownership and control of land.

In spite of their problems, existing industrial land and buildings in the inner cities are an important and often under-used physical resource, and much can be done to improve the operating conditions of those firms that want or need to stay in the inner city. Industrial improvement areas are an attempt to borrow the approach of the housing improvement areas for upgrading the physical environment of industry and commerce in the inner cities, and follow the pioneering work of two northern local authorities: Tyne-and-Wear and Rochdale.

Tyneside has a long tradition of high unemployment levels, dependence on manufacturing industry and socialist local government. It is not surprising, therefore, that as soon as the Tyne-and-Wear Metropolitan County Council was created in 1974, it acted to make the older industrial areas more attractive. A special Act of Parliament, the *Tyne-and-Wear Act* 1976, empowered the council to carry out work and give financial assistance to firms; and an industrial improvement area was created at Green Lane, Pelaw, three miles from Gateshead, on an area of 8.5 hectares (21 acres), part of which the council already owned. On this land a number of pilot projects took place: derelict land reclamation, landscaping and tree planting, construction of nursery factory units to stimulate new small enterprises, improved road access, new drains and other main services. The support of local industrialists and residents was obtained and finance found from the local rates, regional development and derelict land grants and the European Regional Development Fund.

Rochdale has traditions of self-help and active local government, being the home of the co-operative movement (as well as the birth-place of Lancashire entertainer Gracie Fields and the constituency of the entertaining Liberal politician Cyril Smith). In 1974 the newly-created Metropolitan Borough Council adopted a policy of gradual renewal for its obsolete industrial areas, similar to the area improvement approach of GIAs and HAAs. In 1976, after extensive preliminary surveys, it began implementing an action area programme in the Crawford Street Industrial Improvement Area which it had unofficially declared, comprising 51 hectares and some 50 firms, a mile from the town centre. The various projects had three main elements:

(a) Land use changes, including clearing some unfit housing and consolidating industrial uses on land formerly occupied by housing.

(b) Improving open space and pedestrian movement, particularly by clearing and landscaping the long-disused Rochdale Canal with a derelict land grant and Job Creation Programme labour.

(c) Traffic management, with new service roads and accesses constructed by arrangement with the local industrialists.

One of the more exotic experiments explored was the idea of a 'flying derelict land grant', declaring unusable upper floors of mill buildings as statutory derelict land and then obtaining a grant to demolish them and reroof the retained lower floors. Finance came from the European Regional Development Fund, various central and local government grants, local rate funds and private investment by occupying firms and development agencies.

An assessment of the Rochdale experiment commissioned by the Department of the Environment concluded in 1979:

> Overall it is likely that the IIA programme will achieve a major improvement in the economic performance and environmental quality of the area, principally through the reclamation assembly and preparation of land and the generation of confidence. Making land available to meet the expansion and modernization requirements of existing firms in the area is the critical contribution that the Council has made to the development of the area; the cost and complexity of assembling land (and the need for statutory powers) for existing and new firms make it a function that can only be performed by the Council. Confidence in the area and hence the likelihood of investment taking place have been increased by the Council's visible commitment of funds and attention. Residents' environmental expectations will probably be met by the programme; relatively minor traffic management and environmental improvements will be as effective in achieving this as major land use reorganization. The Council's intervention and expenditure have provided the opportunity for major investment of private funds by occupying firms and development agencies (*Time for Industry*, 1979, pp. ii–iii).

The success of the Rochdale IIA was the result of active co-operation by local residents and industrialists, a strong alliance of councillors and officers, a receptive approach by the Manchester regional office of central government, and publicity to encourage private investment. Both Rochdale and Tyne-and-Wear went on to declare further IIAs, and their initiatives were so well received that IIAs became a major part of new inner city legislation.

The *Inner Urban Areas Act* 1978 gave increased powers to inner city local authorities, which the Secretary of State might designate, to assist industry and commerce. The Act enabled designated local authorities to:

(a) Declare improvement areas, either industrial or commercial, subject to the approval of the Secretary of State, in which they can make loans or grants for environmental improvements, and give grants for the conversion and improvement of industrial or commercial buildings of up to 50% of the cost of the works, or £1000 for each job created or preserved.

(b) Make up to 90% loans, on commercial terms, for costs of acquiring land and carrying out building and site works.

(c) Give loans or grants toward the cost of setting up common ownership or co-operative enterprises.

The Act also gave partnership authorities additional powers to make grants and loans to firms taking on new leases of industrial and commercial premises, for site preparation (including demolition of structures or buildings, removal of foundations, clearance and levelling of land), and to small firms employing under 50 staff. Designated authorities were also enabled to adopt local plans before approval of the revelant structure plan. (This was a change to the plan-making procedures under the *Town and Country Planning Act* 1971 so that inner city authorities' plan implementation would not be unnecessarily delayed, and was later incorporated into the *Local Government, Planning and Land Act* 1980.)

Following the Act a number of councils were given designated status, and by mid-1980 the Department of the Environment had processed 56 improvement areas under the Act and was considering another 20. Most were IIAs, although there was an interesting experiment with a shopping improvement area in Wallasey (Merseyside). The Act did not authorize additional finance for designated authorities, and therefore funds came either from the Urban Programme or from the locally determined sector of local government finance. The take-up of grants and loans under the Act has been small, and they have therefore made little contribution to inner city firms' economic viability, but some small-scale local improvements have been achieved, usually servicing

Figure 22 Work in progress on an industrial improvement area, improving vehicle access to existing factories.

arrangements and building modifications. Perhaps as important as the financial resources have been the breaking down of old suspicions and hostilities between councils and local industrialists and businessmen, and the recognition by local authorities that they should be concerned with industrial improvement and the prosperity of their local economy.

Enterprise zones

The Conservative Government's analysis of economic problems emphasizes the role of bureaucratic controls and government fiscal demands in stifling private enterprise and inner city regeneration. Their approach to the inner city has therefore included the concept of enterprise zones, which, by removing those burdens may bring new life back to areas of economic dereliction.

Enterprise zones were not mentioned in the Inner City White Paper of the previous Labour Government, but the idea has been actively discussed for some time. Professor Peter Hall of Reading University, himself a Fabian Socialist, proposed in an article in *New Society* (February 1977) a 'free-port' experiment in 'non-plan', drawing upon the examples of Hong Kong, Singapore and Hamburg. Hall's free-port, which he saw as a 'last-ditch solution to urban problems', would be free of Government controls and taxes (e.g. personal and corporation tax, customs and excise duties, social security, immigration controls, planning and environmental regulations) and Third World businessmen with capital and expertise would be encouraged to invest. The Government Customs and Excise considered that there would be no customs advantages in such proposals, which added little to the bonded warehousing system already existing in Britain. A leading Conservative politician, Sir Geoffrey Howe, took up a modified version of Hall's idea in a speech given in London's Docklands (June 1978), advocating a return to the apparent efficiency and energy of 19th century 'laissez-faire' capitalism, untrammelled by governmental interference.

Howe, then Chancellor of the Exchequer, announced the Conservative Government's proposals for enterprise zones in his budget speech in March 1980. Within enterprise zones new and existing firms would enjoy the following benefits:

(a) Exemption from development land tax.

(b) 100% capital allowances (for corporation and income tax purposes) for commercial and industrial buildings, at an estimated cost of £20 million per annum.

(c) Exemption from general rates on commercial and industrial property, with local authorities reimbursed for their net loss of rate income by 100% specific Exchequer grants (estimated cost £10–15 million per annum).

(d) Simplified planning procedures. A scheme for each enterprise zone would show which classes of development were permitted in each part of the zone, set out any conditions governing development (e.g. health and safety, control of pollution), and specify any 'reserved matters'. After designation, developers would not need to apply for planning permission for developments that conformed with the scheme. They might need local authority approval for 'reserved matters' (e.g. highway access). Approval for developments not conforming with the scheme would need individual application in the normal way, and standards for health and safety at work and pollution control would not be relaxed.

(e) Exemption from Industrial Training Board levies.

(f) Improved handling of requests or customs facilities (e.g. inward processing relief, private customs warehouses).

(g) Abolition of any remaining requirements for an industrial development certificate.

(h) Minimal requests by Government for statistical information.

The main statutory provisions for enterprise zones were subsequently included in the *Local Government, Planning and Land Act* 1980 (Part XVIII and Schedule 32). Under these the Secretary of State could 'invite' any local authority, new town or urban development corporation to prepare a 'scheme' for an enterprise zone, with appropriate public consultation (including a right to question the scheme within six weeks in the High Court). A scheme would define the boundaries of the zone, grant planning permission for certain types of development (subject to specified conditions and exclusions), define rate exemptions and provide a basis for reviews of structure and local plans.

Eleven enterprise zones came into operation during 1981, as follows:

Corby (Northamptonshire)
Dudley (West Midlands)
Hartlepool (Cleveland)
Isle of Dogs (London)
Newcastle and Gateshead (Tyne-and-Wear)
Trafford and Salford (Greater Manchester)
Speke (Merseyside)
Swansea (West Glamorgan)
Wakefield (Yorkshire)
Clydebank (Glasgow)
Belfast (Northern Ireland)

They varied in area from 160 to 430 hectares, with about 200 hectares (500 acres) being the normal size, and each zone usually comprised more than one (up to about seven) separate sites or areas. Enterprise zones were not specifically intended by Government to form part of the inner city policy (e.g. Corby is a new town suffering the consequences of a major steel-works closure), but most of them were near, if not in, inner areas and dock areas of the major cities. After the first eleven zones the Government did not plan any further zones, mainly because of the cost of lost tax revenue and rate reimbursements. Some local authorities supplemented the zone incentives by allocating Inner City Programme funds to promote development in their zones.

The enterprise zone experiment is intended to operate for ten years, and it is early to assess its success or failure, but criticisms have been levelled at the concept from various quarters. In a Parliamentary debate on the subject, Labour MPs called the enterprise zone approach to urban decay 'using a Tiger Moth to reach the moon' and 'a charter for tax evasion'. Others claimed that the zones, as implemented, had been restricted by central government bureaucracy and the original good intentions diluted and frustrated. Professor Peter Hall considered that the zones were closer to regional development areas or new town plans than the idea he had originally proposed, that they would attract firms from neighbouring areas rather than from overseas investors, and that they would fail to meet trading competition from the cheap-labour countries of the Third World. Strong local criticism came from existing commercial and industrial interests near the zones, which resented the competitive advantages those within the zones would enjoy from tax and rate reliefs. Local authorities were concerned that the zones might draw business and vitality from nearby city centres, and affect the viability of committed redevelopment projects. Most of the local authorities invited to prepare schemes, while welcoming any initiative which might alleviate their desperate economic problems, nevertheless sought to keep as much control as possible, fearing a return to the uncontrolled urban development of the 19th century, which town planning and other local government legislation had been passed to prevent.

Even when the zones have been operating for some years, it may be difficult to assess their performance. Not least is the difficulty of measuring effects when one of their advantages is claimed as being minimal requests for statistical information. When consultants were appointed by the Department of the Environment to monitor the development of the zones, their brief required them to submit their information requests to the Central Statistical Office, which would assess the burden they might impose on commerce and industry.

The zones will receive financial benefits similar to regional development grants, and may therefore increase firms' profitability, but the financial benefits may accrue to land-owners through increased land values rather than to the developer or user of the land. Delays in obtaining planning permission have apparently lengthened the period needed to build new factories in Britain (compared, for instance, with Europe or the USA), and relaxations in these controls, as well as exemption from Development Land Tax, will probably help attract new development to the zones. The benefits seem to be most attractive for retail warehouses, and fears have been expressed that the zones will become areas for warehousing or container depots, creating few jobs and exhibiting little in the way of dynamic business enterprise. Some of the enterprise zone schemes, with sensitive local situations, have imposed a relatively low floorspace limit on planning permission for retail units.

The enterprise zone experiment is being watched with interest, both in Britain and abroad, and if successful may be applied elsewhere. It has an emotional appeal to hard-pressed business entrepreneurs, and ultimately its success depends upon the response of the private sector. Unfortunately inner city locations have not in the past attracted corporate investment, especially when economic recession has created surplus land and premises in better locations and reduced the supply of foot-loose industry. The combined incentives offered in enterprise zones may well have only a marginal effect on investment decisions, the local economies and employment creation.

Urban development corporations in the docklands

Since the 1960s the docklands of Britain's ports have been a major element in the redundancy and dereliction of inner areas. The docks were mostly built during the 19th century when Britain led the world in maritime trade. In the early 20th century control of them was consolidated in the hands of a few large companies and undertakers like the Port of London Authority and the Manchester Ship Canal Company. Employment in docks and warehousing tended to be intermittent and unskilled, with a tradition of labour disputes. The inland waterway and canal network was developed to link dock facilities and businesses seeking to reduce transport costs of bulk materials such as timber and furniture. The effect on the docks of the decline in Britain's overseas empire

Figure 23 Dock buildings. The hoisting gear, loading doors and high-level hopper show the difficulty of adapting these multi-storey buildings to modern usage, although this building at least has access for vehicles.

was mitigated by the increased activity of two world wars and post-war reconstruction, but by the late 1960s changes in operational requirements for port facilities (such as for container traffic, increased drafts and tonnages of merchant shipping, and the

Figure 24 St Katherine's Dock, East London, converted to new uses after its closure in the 1960s. The left foreground shows the West Dock and marina, the right foreground the Coronarium, and a part of the Tower Hotel at the extreme right can be seen. Left centre is the Ivory House, right centre Greater London Council housing and the Dickens Inn (see Appendix III).

growth of the petroleum tanker trade) had created many redundant docks and basins, covering large tracts of land and water, as well as drastically reducing demand for dock labour in the inner areas. Most of the enterprise zones were in dock areas, and the Conservative Government's other experiment in solving inner city problems, urban development corporations (UDCs), was reserved for the docklands of London and Merseyside.

The local background to the two UDCs is complex. London's derelict docklands extend over an area of about 8 square miles (a tenth of which is enclosed water), stretching east of the Tower of London on both sides of the river, and mostly owned by public authorities (mainly the Port of London Authority (PLA) and the Gas Board). The PLA has been closing docks (e.g. St. Katherine's, West India, East India, Millwall, Surrey Docks) since the mid-1960s, and while St. Katherine's has been successfully redeveloped, what to do with the remainder has been the subject of political argument for a decade. A planning study, commissioned in 1971 by the Greater London Council and the Department of the Environment, from the consultants Travers Morgan, produced various options, but was unacceptable to the authorities involved. A Docklands Joint Committee was formed, with membership from the Greater London Council and the five docklands boroughs (Greenwich, Lewisham, Newham, Southwark and Tower Hamlets). After further studies and public consultation an ambitious strategic plan was produced in 1976, with proposals for large-scale development on both sides of the river; doubling the population of the docklands for an estimated cost of £2000 million. The Greater London Development Plan proposed three action areas in the docklands (London Docks, East India Dock and Beckton).

The inner city partnerships arrangements made additional Urban Programme resources available for the London docklands, and a number of developments have been and are being undertaken. A district plan was prepared and a major industrial estate developed at Beckton, in the London Borough of Newham, involving a drainage scheme and advance factories. Communications were improved, notably by the opening of new passenger services and stations on existing railway tracks, a new Northern Relief Road and improvements to existing roads on the Isle of Dogs. The London Borough of Southwark and the Greater London Council invited development proposals for their jointly-owned 120 acre site at Surrey Docks, and 15 schemes were submitted and exhibited for public comment in 1980. Subsequently an ambitious scheme by Lysander Estates was accepted, comprising shopping, industry, office, hotel, conference, sport, housing, museum and community facilities, totalling nearly two million square feet of floorspace, to be developed in about six years at an estimated cost of £150 million, and creating an estimated 8000 jobs. Other recent developments in the docklands area have included the News International office building in Wapping and the rehabilitation of original dock warehouses in West India Dock. There was also a proposal by Horace Cutler, a past Conservative leader of the Greater London Council, to offer London as a venue for the Olympic Games, with the docklands as the main development area.

In spite of these development initiatives, the regeneration of London's docklands is a massive task, and the implementation of proposals has been handicapped by the economic recession, lack of resources on the scale required, particularly for public investment in infrastructure, and by disagreements between the various authorities involved.

Merseyside, like London, has experienced a drastic decline in her port facilities, leading to the closure of docks on both the Liverpool and Wirral sides of the Mersey River. Particular areas of under-used land were the South Docks (between Pierhead and Dingle, with a dozen redundant docks, which Merseyside County Council had sought to buy for major redevelopment schemes), land in Birkenhead formerly operated by the Mersey Docks and Harbour Company, and an area adjoining the operational North Docks (where there were opportunities for assembling and servicing sites for port-related industry).

Many concerned with the issues of dockland regeneration, notably the Town and Country Planning Association, felt that the task of regenerating the docklands was not an appropriate one for local authorities to undertake, and they advocated setting up an organization on the model of the New Town Development Cor-

Figure 25 Merseyside Maritime Museum at the Pierhead, creating a tourist attraction in Liverpool's derelict docks.

porations, which had carried out Britain's successful new towns programme after the Second World War. These corporations were public bodies, run by a board of appointed members, staffed by public employees outside central and local government establishments, with large financial resources allocated directly from central government. They had extensive powers but were not subject to the full range of local authority statutory duties and obligations. The Conservative Government in 1974 created a Docklands Development Authority for the London docklands, but its powers and resources were too limited for it to be effective. It was viewed with suspicion by the Labour-controlled London boroughs in the area, while the Greater London Council felt that it, and not a new agency, should have the main strategic role in docklands regeneration. The Inner City White Paper, prepared by a Labour Government, had rejected the idea of UDCs, stating:

> The Government have considered the possibility of using new town style development corporations to tackle inner areas. They could be expected to bring to bear single-minded management, industrial promotional expertise and experience in carrying out development. On the other hand, the task in inner areas is quite different from green field development where there is only a small existing population. Development will be needed, but it will also be a matter of modifying the provision of local authority services and of working with residents to secure the improvement of housing, the environment and community facilities. In the circumstances, it is important to preserve accountability to the local electorate. The Government do not, therefore, propose the establishment of inner city development corporations (p. 8).

The Conservatives came to power in 1979, intending to pursue the UDC idea further, and made provision in the *Local Government, Planning and Land Act* 1980 (Part XVI and Schedules 26–9). In metropolitan districts or inner London boroughs the Secretary of State can designate urban development areas and establish UDCs for them. Membership of a UDC consists of a chairman and vice-chairman, and 5 to 11 members appointed by the Secretary of State. Its objective is 'to secure the regeneration of the area . . . by bringing land and buildings into effective use, encouraging the development of existing and new industry and commerce, creating an attractive environment and ensuring that housing and social facilities are available to encourage people to live and work in the area' (Part XVI). The powers of UDCs are widely drawn, and include: acquiring, holding, managing, reclaiming and disposing of land and other property, carrying out building and other operations, carrying on a business, and to 'generally do anything necessary or expedient for the purposes of the object', subject to Secretary of State control. The Secretary of State can vest land in a UDC held by other public authorities, and UDCs have the powers of a designated authority under the *Inner Urban Areas Act* 1978.

Following the Act two UDCs were created, the Merseyside Development Corporation (MDC) and the London Docklands Development Corporation (LDDC). The first, the MDC, was made responsible for an area of about 350 hectares, including some land vested in it by transfer from other public authorities, and for its first year of operations was allocated £17 million in grants and loans. Its strategy was similar to that of the Merseyside County Council, with the Bootle area a priority for industrial development, and the docks in the south (King's, Queen's, Wapping south to Coburg Dock) deployed mainly for commercial, residential and recreational purposes, including service industry. The establishment of the LDDC was delayed by various complications, including union disagreements over pay and conditions for the new staff, and petitions objecting to the proposed boundaries. In London the Docklands Inner City Partnership arrangements were discontinued, but the new corporation was given responsibility for the Isle of Dogs enterprise zone as an added incentive to investors, as well as grants and loans from central government totalling £100 million in the first year of operation (including £20 million for land purchase).

In Merseyside the prospects for the new UDC were partly overshadowed by the Toxteth riots, just outside its designated area, in the summer of 1981, and by the visit of Environment Secretary Heseltine to the disaffected area. The limitations of a UDC solution to inner city problems were shown by its virtual absence from the 14-point plan for Merseyside which he proposed in August 1981. (The 14 points were: community refurbishing of Council housing estates, private low-cost house-building using apprentices from the unemployed, schools converted into small-firm workshops, information technology centres, local firms to take on more young people and to second managers for job retraining, refurbishing of older industrial estates, £1 million for sports facilities, Knowsley and St Helen's included in vacant land register, Liverpool Maritime Museum to take over part of Albert Dock, possible northern home for Tate Gallery, area near Anglican Cathedral to be redeveloped, more housing association support for house renovation, reclamation of fringe land in St Helen's with Countryside Commission, and training centres for service industry.)

The new corporations differ in several important respects from the new town development corporations on which they were partly modelled. The new town corporations were originally the creation of a Labour Government, under the *New Towns Act* 1946, and therefore were organizations for state intervention, with a large professional staff, wide executive powers, and (at least until recently) generous funding from central government. The UDCs were created by a Conservative Government wanting to by-pass what it saw as slow-moving and indecisive existing local authorities. The new corporations were therefore slimmer organizations, with less than a hundred full-time staff (compared with over a thousand staff at Milton Keynes Development Corporation), and greater reliance on private consultants and contractors for investigating and implementing development projects. While the UDCs were vested with substantial land holdings in their areas, and had (at least on paper) wide-ranging powers, their financial backing from central government was small, and they therefore have to concentrate on a facilitative rather than an executive role. To help attract private investment, the LDDC, for instance, had a property millionaire (Nigel Broackes) as its chairman, while its vice-chairman was the Labour Member of Parliament for Southwark (Bob Mellish), to provide a local connection.

It is early to say whether the UDCs will be more successful in regenerating docklands than previous attempts, but their role in relation to local government has been strongly criticized. Their creation has denied the local strategic authority (Greater London Council or Merseyside County Council) the opportunity to undertake the biggest regeneration project taking place in its area, and yet the new corporations, while they have a variety of development control and other planning functions, do not have the plan-making power under the *Town and Country Planning Act* 1971, which is retained by local government. While the corporations are to prepare a code of practice for consultation arrangements with the relevant local authorities, there seems to be ample scope for disagreement and delay – precisely the problem which UDCs were supposed to avoid. The Labour-controlled dockland London boroughs, in particular, are suspicious of a corporation with appointed, not elected, members, and sceptical whether it will respond to local opinion or to the needs of the local economy. Thus the introduction of a new authority into an already complicated situation is unlikely to make solutions quicker or easier to achieve.

Another problem which the creation of UDCs has not solved is the level of public investment in the infrastructure required, particularly in the London docklands, which connect with two strategic roads, one each side of the river, and both already congested. The relative priorities of improved road communications and a mass rapid-transit system have been disputed between the authorities concerned. In 1980 the Conservative Government cancelled plans for extending the Jubilee underground line into the docklands and for constructing a Southern Relief Road, cutting a proposed investment in docklands transport infrastructure of £760 million over 15 years to £100 million. The future of road and rail communications for the docklands is therefore still uncertain, like other much-needed infrastructure investments (e.g. land reclamation and drainage works). Funds may be available through the European Economic Community, or conceivably from a reallocation of North Sea oil revenues, but the prospects for investment on the scale required are not good.

Conclusions

This chapter has briefly examined the four main experiments in inner city policy since the Inner City White Paper, two introduced by a Labour government, two by a Conservative one. They illustrate the different party approaches: Labour giving the local authorities a key role in partnerships and IIAs, and using public money in the form of grants; while the Conservatives have sought to cut through bureaucratic constraints with enterprise zones and UDCs, and use tax and rate concessions rather than grants as the financial attraction.

All four approaches are based upon selected areas, and are therefore successors to the area improvement and positive discrimination initiatives of the previous decade, reflecting the amorphous nature of inner city problems, their relatively low political importance and the limited resources made available. All four experiments are predominantly concerned with economic regeneration, although not necessarily with creating employment for inner city residents (which is seen as a desirable but secondary concern).

All four are experiments in the machinery of government, rather than in a mixed-sector or community-based approach to inner city problems. All could be said to reflect a managerial approach, being products of a closed rather than open style of government (compared, for instance, with American city government). Even the partnerships, which were intended to support innovative projects through the Urban Programme, do not seem to have drawn upon the potential of local communities or the private sector as much as might have been hoped.

8

Learning from overseas experience

Inner city problems are not unique to Britain. Many of them, e.g. ethnic minorities, economic decline, physical dereliction and multiple deprivation, are found elsewhere, particularly in advanced industrial countries with histories of international trade and a recent slackening of economic activity. While this book is primarily concerned with Britain, the variety of problems and approaches in other countries and the value of exchanging ideas are increasingly being recognized. This chapter will examine experiences in the USA, Europe and the Third World.

An influential attempt to transfer ideas and to learn from the experience of others was made in the Trinational Inner Cities Project (1978–9). This developed from the Habitat Conference at Vancouver in 1977, and involved the Institute for Environment and Development, funding from the German Marshall Fund and research organizations from Germany, the USA and Britain (the British one being the School for Planning Studies, University of Reading) reviewing and exchanging their countries' experience. The central part of the project was called 'the transfer process', in which small teams of practitioners from each country visited their counterparts in other countries to examine their approach to specific inner city problems and discover what could be learned and applied from the experience in their own country. The three main topics examined by the British team were urban economic development, community enterprise and neighbourhood revitalization, and among the lessons for Britain which the project stressed were the need for closer working between public and private sectors, more sophisticated approaches to community enterprise and a wider approach to area improvement of housing.

Inner cities in the United States of America

The closest similarities to the British inner city situation are to be found in the USA. The definitions used, however, vary. For instance, American usage often refers to 'central city' rather than 'inner city' problems, reflecting the more physically dispersed pattern of American conurbations, and also the political problems of local government structure and areas of jurisdiction.

Inner city problems – physical obsolescence, deprivation among the ethnic minorities, declining economy and services – have been recognized for longer in the USA than in Britain, since the Poverty Programme and other Federal Government initiatives by President Johnson in the 1960s, although a specific inner city policy on the lines of the British Inner City White Paper has not been formulated. American cities experienced large-scale post-war redevelopment projects (although not on the scale of the war-damaged British cities) and then public disillusion and reaction against them. The disillusion was symbolized in 1972 with the demolition by blowing-up of the Pruitt-Igoe housing estate after only twenty years of existence; a massive failed experiment in public housing which in its day had won architectural design awards. American cities also experienced declines in population, employment and investment, and the process sometimes described as de-urbanization (similar to the British pattern of suburbanization and decentralization). They also experienced race riots in the late 1960s far worse than those in Britain because of the greater numbers and intense frustrations of ghetto minorities.

Geographically inner city problems similar to Britain's are concentrated in the north-east and north-central regions of the USA, which have lost their traditional manufacturing dominance to other regions (notably to the 'sun-belt' of the south and west), and whose rapid 19th century urban growth and 20th century black immigration has now left a legacy of physical obsolescence and social deprivation. Nathan and Adams' (1976) analysis of 'central city hardship' measured the relationship between the central city and suburban areas of the American conurbations, using six indicators of hardship (unemployment, dependency, educational level, income level, crowded housing and poverty) and found that, when ranked in descending order of hardship, the north-east and north-central regions had most of the top ten deprived central cites (the ten were Newark, Cleveland, Hartford, Baltimore, Chicago, St. Louis, Atlanta, Rochester, Gary, Dayton and New York). Also four of the six American cities with more than a million population (Chicago, New York, Detroit and Philadelphia, but not Los Angeles or Houston) were near the top of the list, all in the north-east or north-central regions.

Some of the differences in the American situation, and lessons for the British inner city situation, can be seen by examining the roles of the agencies – central and local government, private and voluntary sector.

The American governmental system, based on a federation of states, is less centralized than the British system. Thus the complete restructuring of local government (as occurred in Britain in 1974) and a policy of regional development and job dispersal controlled by central government would not be politically possible in the USA. While the Federal Government has attempted to intervene directly in urban problems, notably with the 'Great Society' initiatives of the Kennedy/Johnson Democrat Administration of 1960–8, its success has been limited. The Federal Government, experimenting with corporate planning and Planned Programmed Budgeting Systems (PPBS), created a single Department of Housing and Urban Development (HUD) in 1965 out of previously separate administrative bodies. It embarked upon the Model Cities programme in 1966, aimed at concentrating and co-ordinating resources, and involving local communities in improving living conditions and the physical environment in the cities. The Nixon/Ford Republican Administration of 1968–76 withdrew from these public sector commitments and attempted to involve the private sector more, as the Conservative Government has done in Britain since 1979, through experiments like the 'new towns intown' programme.

While the US Federal Government has a more limited role in

the level of financial support given to local government, its mechanisms for grant aid (particularly the Urban Development Action Grant, UDAG) have attracted some attention in Britain as a different and perhaps transferrable approach. The main federal funding resource for urban development is the Community Development Block Grant, and as a complement to that UDAGs were introduced by the *Housing and Community Development Act* 1977, with initial funding of $400 million per annum. Local authorities can apply for UDAG if they have appropriate levels of distress on at least three of six defined indicators (low *per capita* income, low population growth, high unemployment rates, low employment growth, old housing stock, high proportions of poverty). The grant is to promote economic and neighbourhood revitalization through innovatory projects with joint public/private-sector finance and community support. UDAG attempts to compensate for the higher development costs on inner city sites by restoring 'parity of profitability' for the private sector, a technique of 'leveraging' similar to the British term 'pump-priming', whereby public money is put into a project to attract private funds and jointly make the project viable.

At the local government level differences between British and American experience are apparent, particularly in the intensity and competitiveness of city politics in the USA. The American city has been called ungovernable (a term which has hardly been used in the British context, at least not yet), because 'the urban policy-making system is incapable of producing coherent decisions, developing effective policies, or implementing state or federal programs' (Yates, 1978, p. 5). The pluralism of the American political system, with a multitude of competing political interests, has become in cities what Yates has called 'street-fighting pluralism . . . a political free-for-all, a pattern of unstructured, multilateral conflict in which many different combatants fight continuously with one another in a very great number of permutations and combinations' (p. 34). American city government depends upon locally-raised rates and taxes more than the British, and therefore economic and population decline, combined with the high costs of providing public services, have direct financial effects on the residents, who put political pressure on the city government. Experiments with enlarged city boundaries and metropolitan authorities have been attempted, notably in the

Minneapolis–St. Paul conurbation, but generally American central cities have had little help from their surrounding suburbs or state governments, reluctant to 'reward laggards', and it took the bankruptcy of the New York City Government to highlight the financial problem of the central cities.

The private sector has been more active in American inner cities than in Britain hitherto, reflecting the stronger local loyalties and linkages of banks and corporations (a result partly of legal restrictions on inter-state banking, and of the vigorous business promotion policies in each state). Also the mutual suspicion between public and private sectors in Britain is less marked in the USA, with freer movement of staff between public and private sector jobs, and closer involvement of the business community in local politics. The Federal Government has actively promoted private sector involvement in the inner cities through UDAG and the 'new town intown' programme. The *Urban Growth and Community Development Act* 1970 provides federal mortgage guarantees to increase the availability of private mortgage fund capital for new urban development projects, particularly for 'race and income integrated communities'. Joint venture urban development corporations have been active for many years, the Philadelphia Development Corporation (holding $1000 million of real estate) being one of the largest and oldest, and these combine public and private sector resources to develop large vacant land parcels near central business districts, or to rehabilitate existing buildings and areas for mixed housing, commercial and industrial uses. One of the most ambitious programmes for regenerating the deprived areas of a city region has been the Hartford Process, begun in the 1960s, whereby the Greater Hartford Community Development Corporation is undertaking large-scale redevelopment and improvement in an area of 750 square miles and 700 000 population, an initiative comparable with the British inner city partnerships but with a larger private sector financial involvement and a more commercial approach. Such a joint venture approach requires skilful financial 'packaging' to make proposals acceptable to a range of potential contributors, and depends upon identifying areas which offer some potential for regeneration. This contrasts with the British approach of concentrating on the worst areas first, which Americans see as unpractical and wasteful of resources.

The voluntary or community sector has also been more active in American inner city regeneration, and for a longer period, than in Britain. This is largely because ethnic minority groups in the USA are older established and form a larger proportion of the total population than in Britain. The main wave of immigration to Britain was after the Second World War, but in the USA since the 18th and 19th century slave trade. In Britain immigrants comprise only about 2.5% of the population, while in the USA blacks are over 10% and Hispanics about 5%, to mention only the two major ethnic minority groups. Such groups, largely excluded by discrimination from the formal sector of employment, have long practised self-help within their own communities, and since the ghetto riots of the late 1960s American community development initiatives have proliferated, with or without government assistance. The scale of some such community businesses dwarfs comparable ventures in Britain: Goodwill Industries of Southern California, which repairs and sells discarded personal items, had a turnover of $6 million in 1978 and employed some 900 people. Again financial packaging is important, how to 'nickle and dime', combining evangelical private fund-raising with 'grantsmanship' to attract public funds. Similar training funds to those of the Manpower Services Commission's special programmes are administered by the Federal Government, enabling community businesses to retain trading surpluses and equipment in the early stages. Local savings may be ploughed back into the local economy through credit unions.

Housing area improvement shows the differences between the British and American inner city situations and approaches. While British concepts of the housing market have stressed the rigidities of the various housing 'classes', in America the more optimistic concept of a 'filtering' process has been proposed, whereby all social groups improve their housing position by upward mobility through the housing markets (although ethnic minority groups, particularly blacks, may find themselves excluded from this filtering process by racial discrimination and red-lining policies). This filtering process may encourage an over-supply of housing (between 1963 and 1976, 27 million new housing units were built in the USA, but only 17 million new households came into existence, according to Berry, 1980), and it also leads to large-scale abandonment of older inner city housing, particular tenement blocks, as demand for them declines. While in Britain vacant housing stock has been attributed largely to public institutional owners and to inefficiencies in public sector redevelopment programmes, in the USA 'abandonment' seems to be mainly by private company landlords, finding such properties uneconomic to let and manage. The process of 'gentrification', middle-class households moving into inner city areas and displacing previous private tenants, has also occurred in the USA, although apparently more recently than in Britain. It is usually called 'displacement' and is seen as an important mechanism for neighbourhood revitalization.

The American equivalent of British housing improvement areas has been the Neighbourhood Housing Service programme, originating in Pittsburgh and now widely sponsored by HUD and the recently established Neighbourhood Reinvestment Corporation. It is a partnership of residents, local government and private financial institutions, concerned with housing development and rehabilitation, environmental improvement, and promoting self-help and owner-occupation. The areas chosen are larger than British GIAs and HAAs (usually about five thousand dwellings), have at least 50% owner-occupation and must offer potential for revitalization. The board of directors includes a numerical majority of residents. Local financial institutions are involved (through revolving funds, mortgages, etc.) and public funds providing 'leveraging' are supplied to achieve the area's revitalization or 'turn-around'. 'Homesteading' to rehabilitate derelict housing and increase owner-occupation was pioneered by the City of Baltimore's 'dollar homes', and has been extended to commercial properties in run-down areas ('shopsteading').

Those concerned with inner city policy in Britain have become increasingly interested in the US experience. In 1979 the Conservative-controlled Greater London Council sent its leader and other representatives to the USA to examine their approaches in New York, Boston and elsewhere. They stressed certain instructive differences: the more active role of business and commerce, the smaller and less complicated executive structures, the more vigorous marketing of development appraisals, the greater variety of financial incentives and funding packages. The Inner Cities Directorate of the Department of the Environment was involved in the Trinational Inner Cities Project and in relating its findings to the British situation: for instance, American experience in community involvement was particularly relevant to enterprise trusts and similar 'corporate social responsibility activities' being promoted in Britain, and the structuring of community groups into a single, comprehensive and financially sensitive Community Development Corporation on an American model has been advocated. In 1980 an Anglo-American conference on community involvement, held at Sunningdale Park, explored the theme that 'the socio-economic well-being of the community is accepted as a corporate responsibility of both business and government'.

European experience

European experience is less relevant than American to Britain, largely because Britain is more urbanized and has more complex and older urban problems than the rest of Europe. Of the ten largest conurbations in Europe, five (London, Birmingham, Manchester, Glasgow and Leeds/Bradford) are in Britain, the rest being Paris, the Ruhr, Rome, Hamburg and Stuttgart. Furthermore, many European cities were even more extensively rebuilt after the destruction of the Second World War than in Britain, so that the problems of physical dereliction and poor housing are less marked. Nevertheless, there are certain areas of comparison.

What in Britain are called ethnic minorities, in Europe are more usually called migrant workers. It is unofficially estimated that there may be as many as 15 million migrant workers and their dependants in Europe (including Britain), of whom perhaps a tenth are illegal immigrants. In 1974 West Germany acknowledged having 2.3 million migrant workers (a tenth of the economically active population), mainly from Turkey, Yugoslavia and Italy; and France acknowledged 1.9 million, mainly from Spain, Portugal and former North African dependencies. Most of the ethnic minorities in Britain came originally from British dependencies (New Commonwealth and Pakistan), but a similar past affects only a few European countries, notably France (immigrants from Africa and the Far East) and the Netherlands (immigrants from Indonesia). Most migrant workers in Europe come from the poorer Mediterranean countries on the southern periphery, and are likely to retain the nationality of their country of origin, which creates problems of social security entitlement in the host country and rights of entry for their families. The Economic and Social Committee of the European Economic Community (EEC) is responsible for an action programme for migrant workers, which seeks to improve living conditions, education and information services, and to eliminate discrimination. Of relevance in the inner city context is the improvement of older housing in the areas where migrant workers are concentrated, and particularly the use of various forms of housing association and employer's obligation to house.

Regional policy in Europe has not formulated a significant inner city dimension and is concerned with much broader geographical imbalances in economic development. The principal instrument of European regional policy is the European Regional Development Fund (ERDF) (created in 1975), which provides funds for about half of the EEC's territory, containing 100 million of the EEC's 250 million population (before the entry of Greece). Nearly half of Britain's population lives in areas qualifying for ERDF assistance, and its funds are used to boost member states' own regional programmes.

Among the differences in European institutional structures relevant to an inner city context, the following can be mentioned: greater flexibility in housing tenure types (e.g. in tenement blocks, and the large and formalized housing associations of West Germany); mixed-use zonings in town plans; industrial co-operatives and co-ownership schemes; and mixed-sector financing of local development projects (e.g. the chambers of commerce and joint venture corporations in West Germany).

Recognition of some of the urban problems which in Britain are associated with the inner city led to the European Campaign for Urban Renaissance (1980–2), organized by the Council of Europe in its 21 member states. Under the slogan, 'A better life in towns', the campaign had five main themes:

(a) The improvement of urban environmental quality.

(b) The rehabilitation of existing and older buildings, housing and areas.

(c) The provision of social, cultural and economic opportunities.

(d) The achievement of community development and participation.

(e) The role of local authorities.

Using a similar approach to the European Architectural Heritage Year (1977), a campaign was organized through national committees, conferences and a programme of demonstration projects. In Britain this comprised Durham's good husbandry project, Glasgow's Woodlands project, Greater Manchester's Impact campaign, London's Covent Garden Market and reclamation in the Lower Swansea valley.

Third World cities

Third World experience is not usually considered particularly relevant for inner city problems, mainly because Third World cities are still receiving large-scale immigration. A deteriorating urban fabric left over from 19th century urban development can be found in certain former colonial cities, like Lagos, Calcutta or Singapore, usually administrative centres or the ports through which primary produce passed to supply the metropolitan economy. But certain key elements of the inner city situation are lacking, notably decentralization and dispersal policies, and interventionist local government. Certain aspects of the Third World urban situation do, however, make interesting comparisons in an inner city context.

The division between formal, large-scale, and informal, small-scale economic activity is more apparent in Third World than in advanced industrial countries. The large organizations, companies or parastatal bodies, using capital intensive production methods, export-orientated, with Western trained management and data handling, can be contrasted with the small-scale enterprises, requiring little start-up capital, labour-intensive, responding to local economic conditions. Activities like waste reprocessing and community self-help are deeper rooted in these societies, and different approaches have been developed: the organized urban land invasions of Latin America, squatter settlement upgrading in Indian cities, making do with minimal services and infrastructure. Little or nothing is expected, either from central or local government, or from private financial institutions, and therefore community thrift and self-help organizations have to fill the gap. Perhaps, as Britain becomes poorer, the experience and approaches adopted in the cities of Third World poor countries will become increasingly relevant to her inner city problems.

9

A future for the inner city

Problems and perceptions of the inner city situation constantly change. The adverse effects of rising unemployment and structural changes in the economy have overtaken the approach of tackling localized pockets of urban deprivation, with which inner city policy began in the early 1970s. Also less is said now about the role of local government and the local agencies of central government than at the time of the Inner City White Paper in 1977. Now that both Labour and Conservative governments have had the opportunity to present their remedies for inner city ills, it is perhaps appropriate to prepare a balance sheet for the last few years of activity on inner city regeneration.

On the credit side, the population decline of the inner city may have moderated. A more stable and balanced population structure may be emerging, with a greater mixture than before of socio-economic, ethnic and housing tenure groups. Also, there are less marked contrasts of population and employment densities from the outer areas, compared with a decade ago. Institutions have adapted, if slowly, to the realities of the inner city situation. For instance, financial institutions are more willing than a few years ago to support projects and to mortgage properties in the inner areas, and local planning authorities have become more tolerant of nonconformity and more flexible in their plan-making. Also the public and private sectors are now more willing to co-operate with each other in new ventures (such as industrial improvement areas and enterprise zones). New voluntary and community-based organizations have developed, particularly concerned with environmental improvement and employment creation, and a more flexible government machinery for funding experimental and innovative projects has emerged through the Urban Programme. The physical environment has been improved, with vacant land and buildings being put to new, if temporary, uses, the removal of some of the worst dereliction, and more colour and visual stimulus in the street-scene. Some new development has taken place, more sensitive to local needs than the sweeping redevelopment of the 1960s, for instance, small-unit advance factories. Rehabilitation and conversion, of both residential and non-residential properties, has become more sophisticated and efficient.

On the debit side, much of the inner city situation seems to have worsened, not improved. The economic state has deteriorated, with more unemployment and firm closures. The inner city seems to have fared worse than the outer parts of the conurbations and the rest of the country. The position of ethnic minorities, particularly the West Indians, has deteriorated, and warnings about police persecution of ethnic minorities and imminent racial conflict seem to be more frequent. Public sector investment, particularly the level of local services, has deteriorated in the inner areas, and the financial burdens on inner city residents, particularly through the rates and public transport fares, have increased. Area-based improvement in housing, economic and other fields, seems to have failed to make any significant, or even palliative, change. Indeed, the major urban problems seem as intractable as ever, and policies of inner city regeneration largely irrelevant to them.

This negative view is supported by the results of the 1981 population census and the increase in inner city disorder after 1980. The 1981 census showed that smaller towns and rural areas were more economically buoyant than the cities, while the depopulation of the large cities continued (with inner London boroughs losing up to a quarter of their residents since 1971). The inner city riots showed a frustration among inner city residents, particularly the young and black, after a decade of platitudes and programmes. The causes offered for the riots varied and sometimes contradicted each other according to political stance; too little policing or too aggressive policing, too little parental discipline or too much parental oppression, failures at home or failures at school, too few jobs or too many work-shy youngsters. A consensus view of the problems and their solutions seem as far away as ever.

As for the prospects of the inner cities, both major political parties are agreed that Britain cannot have a regenerated economy with the inner cities rotting at the heart of it, although the solutions they propose differ, particularly in the emphasis given to the public and private sectors. There is unlikely to be any major capital investment, either public or private, in the inner cities for some years (with the possible exception of docklands), and, when it comes, improving mobility is likely to be a priority. In the meantime, the release of land and buildings held by public authorities as well as more flexible planning attitudes to mixed uses, may help promote new community-based activities which hitherto have been hampered because of the low financial yield they offer the property-owner. Unemployment will probably remain high, especially among the poorly educated and disadvantaged, and different organizational styles, essentially small-scale, will develop to deploy these under-used human resources in community self-help and in reprocessing land and materials. The mechanisms for grant-aiding community enterprises may improve, and technological improvements in information exchange and more adaptive educational styles may assist the spread of innovative schemes. Multi-national agencies, such as the European Regional Development Fund, may also become more important as sources of funding.

Conceivably Government revenues from North Sea oil could be deployed for a much-needed rebuilding of the inner city infrastructure. The differences between inner and outer areas of the conurbations, particularly in the physical mix and density of population and employment, are likely to reduce, so that the special characteristics of the inner city situation will be less distinguishable. Perhaps the inner city problem will not so much be solved, as be redefined out of existence.

References and further reading

Chapter 1 (General studies)

There are three useful series of publications dealing with aspects of inner city problems: the *Inner Cities in Context* series (Social Science Research Council, London, 1980), the *Inner Cities Research Programme* series (Department of the Environment, London, from 1980 onwards), and various *Working Papers* of the School of Advanced Urban Studies, University of Bristol, from 1979 onwards, based on a series of Inner City Workshops held by the School in 1979–80.

Cameron, G. (ed.), *The Future of the British Conurbations: Policies and Prescriptions for Change* (Longmans, London, 1980).

Community Development Programme, *Gilding the Ghetto: The State and the Poverty Experiments* (London, 1977).

Department of the Environment, *Inner Area Studies: Summaries of Consultants Final Report* (London, 1977).

Edwards, J. and Batley, R., *The Politics of Positive Discrimination: An Evaluation of the Urban Programme 1967–77* (Tavistock, London, 1978).

HMSO, *Policy for the Inner Cities* (Command 6845, 1977).

Holterman, S. *Census Indicators of Urban Deprivation*, Department of the Environment, working note 6 (1975).

Jones, C. (ed.), *Urban Deprivation and the Inner City* (Croom Helm, London 1979).

Lawless, P., *Urban Deprivation and Government Initiative* (Faber, London, 1979).

Loney, M. and Allan, M. (ed.), *The Crisis of the Inner City* (Macmillan, London, 1979).

Mackay, D.H. and Cox, A.W., *The Politics of Urban Change* (Croom Helm, London, 1979).

Chapter 2 (Agencies)

Bailey, J., *Social Theory for Planning* (Routledge and Kegan Paul, London, 1975).

Burgess, T. and Travers, T., *Ten Billion Pounds: Whitehall's takeover of the Town Halls* (Grant Macintyre, London, 1980).

Cadman, D., Private Capital and the Inner City, *Estates Gazette* No. 249 (1979) 1257–60.

Kennett, S., Local Government Fiscal Problems: A Context for Inner Areas, *Inner Cities in Context* (Social Science Research Council, London, 1980).

Morley, D. *et al.*, *Making Cities Work: The Dynamics of Urban Innovation* (Croom Helm, London, 1980).

Pearce, J. and Cassidy, P. *Can We Make Jobs* (BBC, London, 1980).

Rock, D., *The Grassroot Developers: A Handbook for Town Development Trusts* (RIBA, London, 1979).

Slough Estates Ltd, *The Inner City: A Location for Industry?* (1977).

Tunley, P., Travers, T. and Pratt, J., *Depriving the Deprived: A Study of Finance, Educational Provision and Deprivation in a London Borough* (Kogan Page, London, 1979).

Wolfenden Committee Report, *The Future of Voluntary Organizations* (HMSO, London, 1978).

Chapter 3 (Planning)

Best, R.H. and Coppock, J.T., *The Changing Use of Land in Britain* (Faber, London, 1962).

Bishop, D. *et al.*, *Underground Services in the Inner City* (Inner Cities Research Project Publication 3, Department of the Environment, 1979).

Burrows, J.W., Vacant Urban Land: A Continuing Crisis, *The Planner,* January (1978).

Civic Trust, *Urban Wasteland: A Report on Land Lying Dormant in Cities, Towns and Villages in Britain* (London, 1977).

Department of the Environment, *Industry in the Inner City: Case Studies of Mixed Use Redevelopment* (London 1978).

Manners, G., Regional Policy Rethink, *Town and Country Planning* (1976) 208–14.

McKean, C. *Fight Blight: A Practical Guide to the Causes of Urban Dereliction and What People Can Do About It* (Kaye and Ward, London, 1977).

Royal Town Planning Institute, *Land Values and Planning in the Inner Areas* (Report of working party, London, 1978).

Chapter 4 (Economic regeneration)

Barrett, S. and Boddy, M. (ed.), *Local Authority/Private Sector Industrial Partnerships* (School of Advanced Urban Studies Working Paper 18, University of Bristol, Bristol, 1981).

Bosanquet, N. and Doeringer, P., Is There a Dual Labour Market in Great Britain?, *Economic Journal,* **83** (1973) 421–35.

English Tourist Board, *Tourism and the Inner City* (London, 1980).

Evans, A. and Eversley, D. (ed.), *The Inner City: Employment and Industry* (Heinemann, London, 1980).

Goddard, J.B. and Thwaites, A.T., *Technological Change and the Inner City* (Social Science Research Council, London, 1980).

Hart, D.A. *Strategic Planning in London: The Rise and Fall of the Primary Road Network* (Pergamon, Oxford, 1976).

Jacobs, J., *The Economy of Cities* (Penguin, London, 1970).

Keeble, D., Industrial Decline in the Inner City and Conurbation, *Transactions of the Institute of British Geographers,* **3** (1978) 101–11.

Rogers, P.B. and Smith, C.R., The Local Authority's Role in Economic Development – *The Tyne-and-Wear Act* 1976, *Regional Studies*, **11** (1977) 153–63.
Schumacher, E., *Small is Beautiful* (Blond and Briggs, London, 1973).
Use of Redundant Buildings, series in *Architects Journal* (from February 1978).
Williams, H. *et al.*, *Industrial Renewal and the Inner City – An Assessment of Potential and Problems* (Inner City Research Programme, Department of the Environment, 1980).

Chapter 5 (Housing)

Lansley, S., *Housing and Public Policy* (Croom Helm, London, 1979).
Needleman, L., *The Economics of Housing* (Staples, London, 1965).
Paris, C. and Blackaby, R., *Not Much Improvement* (Heinemann, London, 1979).
Rex, J. and Moore, R., *Race, Community and Conflict* (Institute of Race Relations, London, 1967).
Stafford, D.C., *The Economics of Housing* (Croom Helm, London, 1976).
Weir, S., Red-Line Districts, *Roof*, (1976).
Williams, P., *Building Societies and the Inner City* (Centre for Urban and Regional Studies Research Memorandum 54, Birmingham, 1977).
Wohl, A.S., *The Eternal Slum* (Edward Arnold, London, 1977).

Chapter 6 (Social provision)

City and Hackney Community Health Council, *Homeless and Healthless – Health Care for Single Homeless People in an Inner City Health District* (London, 1980).
Cross, C., *Ethnic Minorities in the Inner City*, (Commission for Racial Equality, London, 1978).
Department of the Environment, *Recreation and Deprivation in Inner Urban Areas* (London, 1977).
Eversley, D. and Bonnerjea, L., *Changes in the Resident Populations of Inner Areas* (Social Science Research Council, London, 1980).
Manpower Services Commission and Commission for Racial Equality, *Special Programmes Special Needs: Ethnic Minorities and the Special Programmes for the Unemployed* (London, 1979).
Plowden, Lady, *Children and their Primary Schools* (HMSO, London, 1967).
Roberts, J., *A Review of Studies of Sport and Recreation in the Inner City* (Sports Council Study 17, London, 1978).
Tunley, P., Travers, T. and Pratt, J., *Depriving the Deprived: A Study of Finance, Educational Provision and Deprivation in a London Borough* (Kogan Page, London, 1979).

Chapter 7 (Four governmental experiments)

Denyer-Green, B., The *Local Government, Planning and Land Act* 1980, *Estates Gazette*, **257** (1981) 369, 371–2.
Docklands Joint Committee, *A Strategy for Docklands* (1976).
Department of the Environment, *Time for Industry* (London, 1979).
Department of the Environment, *Partnership in Action* (London, 1981).
Nabarro, R. and McDonald, I., The Urban Programme, *Planner* (1978) 171–4.
Young, M. *et al.*, *Report from Hackney – A Study of an Inner City Area* (Policy Studies Institute, London, 1981).

Chapter 8 (Overseas experience)

Berry, B.J., Inner City Futures – An American Dilemma Revisted, *Transactions of the Institute of British Geographers*, **5, 1,** (1980) 1–28.
Clay, P.L., *Neighbourhood Renewal* (Lexington Books, Massachusetts, 1979).
Hart, D.A., *Urban Economic Development* (University of Reading, Reading, 1980).
Huntly, J., *Neighbourhood Revitalization* (University of Reading, Reading, 1980).
Kirwan, R., *The Inner City in the United States* (Social Science Research Council, London, 1980).
Nathan, R.P. and Adams, C., Understanding Central City Hardship, *Political Science Quarterly*, **91** (1976) 47–62.
Newnham, R., *Community Enterprise* (University of Reading, Reading, 1980).
Perloff, H.S. *et al.*, *Modernizing the Central City* (Ballinger Publications, Cambridge, Massachusetts, 1975).
Yates, D. *The Ungovernable City* (MIT Press, Cambridge, Massachusetts, 1978).

Appendix I

Selected statistics and indicators

Statistical indicators of inner city problems and the inner city condition are difficult to devise for various reasons. Interpretations of the geographical boundaries of inner areas vary, and have to be related to the different data collection areas available, while the complexities of socio-economic conditions cannot always be quantified. Resources are scarce and data collection is often given a low priority (as when the 1976 sample census was cancelled), and the detailed results of the 1981 census were not available at the time of going to press. This appendix therefore restricts itself to a few indicators of the problems.

Table 1 presents four variables, with some attempt at time series, comparing inner areas with other cities and parts of conurbations. Table 2 draws upon the valuable work of Holtermann relating a number of indicators of deprivation by geographical groupings of enumeration districts from the 1971 census. Table 3 adopts a different approach to presenting similar deprivation indicators. Table 4 presents more detailed selected data on London, since that conurbation has the largest inner city population in Britain. Disagreements between the data (for instance, between Tables 3 and 4 on inner London populations) illustrate the difficulty of agreeing definitions and boundaries.

Table 1 Central cities: comparative data (aggregated)

	Rate of population change (%)				*Population density (persons per hectare)*		*Employment decline* (%)	% *of households having no car*
	1921–31	*1931–51*	*1951–61*	*1961–71*	*1961*	*1974*	*1961–71*	*1971*
Greater London conurbation	+9.7	+ 1.6	−2.0	− 8.9	52	45	15.0	53.7
Central cities of other 6 conurbations	+5.6	+ 0.1	−2.9	−12.2	51	42	17.9 (6 + Inner London)	66.8
Outer areas of other 6 conurbations	+3.5	+ 8.8	+5.9	+ 5.8	17	18	5.1 (6 + Inner London)	49.8
12 large non-conurbation cities (population >200 000)	+4.6	+ 6.1	+0.8	− 4.2	35	35 }	4.0 (this and next row)	49.1 (this and next row)
Rest of Great Britain	+3.2	+14.1	+9.0	+12.6	n.a.	n.a. }		

Source: Census data in Cameron (1980).

Table 2 Geographical distribution of enumeration districts with levels of two or more kinds of deprivation exceeding special cut-off values. Per cent in each country, conurbation and regional remainder

Area	*Households overcrowded (1.5 people per room). Male unemployment*		*Households overcrowded. Lack of exclusive use of all basic amenities*		*Male unemployment. Lack of exclusive use of all basic amenities*		*Households overcrowded. Male unemployment. Lack of exclusive use of all basic amenities*		*Enumeration districts exceeding 1% cut-off value of one or more of eleven indicators*
	15%	*5%*	*15%*	*5%*	*15%*	*5%*	*15%*	*5%*	
England	54.7	27.7	76.4	41.9	73.1	54.3	63.2	22.4	61.3
Wales	1.6	0.3	0.7	0.1	6.5	2.4	1.2	0.2	2.4
Scotland	43.8	71.9	22.8	58.1	20.5	43.2	35.6	77.4	36.3
London Group A (inner)	11.7	3.9	37.1	24.4	12.0	3.0	18.1	3.5	20.1
London Group B (outer)	1.1	0.4	6.7	2.0	1.2	0.1	1.4	0.2	3.4
Tyneside	4.6	3.5	1.8	0.6	4.6	6.1	3.2	1.3	4.3
West Yorkshire	4.4	3.1	4.1	3.5	4.5	3.2	5.9	3.3	2.4
Merseyside	5.2	3.9	1.4	0.6	6.7	5.9	2.9	1.1	4.8
SE Lancashire	5.4	3.1	4.4	1.3	8.9	7.7	6.7	1.7	5.6
West Midlands	5.6	4.3	7.4	6.6	5.6	5.6	8.4	8.1	3.3
Clydeside	28.6	56.1	14.9	47.9	14.2	34.2	26.6	68.1	24.7
Rest of south-east area	2.5	0.8	3.3	0.3	3.2	1.0	2.9	0.4	2.0
Rest of northern area	4.4	1.6	2.2	0.8	6.6	7.8	3.6	1.3	3.6
Rest of Yorkshire and Humberside	1.4	0.3	1.1	0.1	5.6	5.3	1.2	0.2	4.4
Rest of north-west area	2.5	1.3	1.3	0.2	4.5	3.4	1.7	–	2.2
Rest of West Midlands	0.1	0.3	1.3	0.5	1.9	0.9	1.4	0.6	0.7
East Midlands	2.2	0.7	3.2	0.8	5.0	3.6	4.2	0.6	2.0
East Anglia	0.4	0.1	0.3	0.1	1.2	0.4	0.4	–	0.4
South-west	1.6	0.5	0.9	0.2	1.7	0.4	1.3	0.4	2.0
Rest of Scotland	15.1	15.8	8.0	10.1	6.2	9.1	9.0	9.4	11.7
Numbers of EDs in overlap areas	5746	1536	5408	1185	4527	1103	2415	545	4684
Percentage of all EDs	6.6	1.8	6.2	1.4	5.2	1.3	2.8	0.6	5.3
Percentage of maximum possible	43.7	35.1	41.2	27.1	34.5	25.2	18.4	12.4	–

Source: Holtermann (1976).

Table 3 Comparative selected indicators of inner city problems in England

Indicator	*Newcastle*		*Manchester*		*Liverpool*		*Birmingham*		*Nottingham*		*London*	
	Inner area	*Conur-bation*	*Inner area*	*Conur-bation*	*Inner area*	*Conur-bation*	*Inner area*	*Conur-bation*	*Inner area*	*Conur-bation*	*Inner area*	*Conur-bation*
Population (thousands)												
1961	268	1622	657	2482	741	1759	1105	2376	311	959	3189	7997
1971	221	1599	546	2465	605	1755	1013	2372	289	1020	2758	7452
% change 1961–71	−17.5	−1.4	−16.9	−0.7	−18.4	−0.2	−8.3	−0.2	−4.2	+6.4	−13.5	−6.8
Age distribution (% in each group)												
1961: 0–14	23.6	25.0	24.3	27.4	26.0	26.2	23.5	22.3	23.9	23.5	19.4	20.2
15–59/64	52.0	61.6	62.1	58.1	61.6	60.5	63.9	64.3	62.3	62.9	65.8	65.2
60/65+	14.4	13.4	13.7	14.5	12.3	13.3	12.4	12.3	13.8	13.7	14.8	14.7
1971: 0–14	23.1	24.2	24.5	24.5	25.1	26.1	24.6	24.7	24.8	24.5	20.1	21.5
15–59/64	59.4	60.1	59.2	59.4	59.2	58.7	60.7	61.0	59.4	60.2	63.5	62.5
60/65+	18.0	15.7	16.4	16.0	15.7	15.1	14.8	14.2	15.8	15.2	16.4	16.4
New Commonwealth immigration (% immigrants in total population)												
1961	0.68	0.28	1.22	0.45	0.54	0.39	1.75	1.49	1.66	1.73	n.a.	0.24
1971	1.28	0.55	3.18	1.34	0.89	0.64	6.73	5.04	3.61	n.a.	n.a.	4.79
Socio-economic composition of economically active males												
1961: Employed, manual, professional	11.8	11.5	9.8	13.3	10.1	12.2	10.1	13.7	9.7	13.9	12.7	16.8
other non-manual	18.9	16.5	18.2	17.6	16.7	18.0	14.6	14.0	15.6	16.4	21.9	23.7
skilled manual	42.5	44.4	43.2	42.3	38.2	37.4	47.2	47.3	44.1	44.1	36.7	36.0
semi/unskilled	26.9	27.6	28.8	26.8	35.1	32.4	28.2	25.0	30.6	26.6	28.7	23.7

1971: Employed, manual,												
professional	12.6	12.4	12.6	n.a.	10.8	n.a.	14.5	19.0	11.3	13.9	16.7	20.6
other non-manual	18.8	18.2	18.3	n.a.	17.4	n.a.	14.5	8.2	15.6	20.3	23.3	24.2
skilled manual	41.0	41.0	42.7	n.a.	38.1	n.a.	42.7	44.0	44.3	40.4	33.7	34.0
semi/unskilled	27.7	28.4	26.4	n.a.	33.5	n.a.	28.3	29.3	28.9	25.4	26.5	21.3
Tenure: % of total households in each tenure group												
1961: Owner-occupied	27.3	28.2	29.3	44.2	24.3	32.1	n.a.	38.1	23.9	35.9	16.6	36.3
public-rented	27.6	32.8	25.2	21.9	27.9	26.8	n.a.	35.4	33.2	26.7	19.5	18.2
private-rented	42.8	36.0	42.4	31.1	45.5	38.4	n.a.	23.5	34.0	32.4	60.6	42.4
1971: Owner-occupied	28.3	32.2	33.4	51.0	31.7	39.9	42.3	45.3	26.5	41.2	19.4	40.4
public-rented	41.0	42.2	35.5	29.7	26.2	33.4	38.2	39.6	45.2	30.8	30.3	24.9
private-rented	30.7	25.5	30.9	19.2	32.0	27.3	19.5	15.1	27.9	22.5	49.2	34.1

Source: Roberts (1979).

Table 4 Selected statistics on London

(a) *Population*

Area	*1961*	*1976*	*% change*
Inner London	3 198 000	2 500 000	−22
Outer London	4 794 000	4 528 000	−6

(b) *Causes of population change: rates per 1000*

Cause	*Area*	*1965/6*	*1975/6*
Natural increase/decrease	Inner London	8.8	−1.0
	Outer London	6.0	−0.2
Net migration	Inner London	−18.4	−17.2
	Outer London	−7.3	−5.4

(c) *Ethnic origin: partnership areas (PA) and Greater London totals (GLT), (% 1978)*

Ethnic origin	*PA*	*GLT*
White	76.4	85.9
West India	11.0	4.1
Africa	2.5	0.9
Indian Sub Continent	2.4	4.1
Other	7.7	5.0

(d) *Socio-economic grouping of all persons economically active: partnership areas (PA) and Greater London totals (GLT) (% 1978)*

Socio-economic group	*PA*	*GLT*
Professional/managerial	10.1	17.2
Other non-manual	32.5	37.9
Skilled manual	24.6	21.9
Semi-skilled manual	19.6	14.7
Unskilled manual	9.0	5.4
Others	4.2	3.0

(e) *Male unemployment rates (% of economically active)*

Area	*1971*	*1974*	*1978*
Inner London	3.6	3.0	7.5
Outer London	1.9	1.6	3.8

(f) *Housing tenure: partnership areas (PA) and Greater London totals (GLT) (% 1978)*

Housing tenure	*PA*	*GLT*
Owned outright	5.7	16.9
Mortgage/loan	8.2	27.6
Rented council	53.2	30.6
Rented housing association	6.2	3.4
Rented private furnished	9.1	7.3
Rented private unfurnished	17.0	14.2

Source: Eversley and Bonnerjea (1980).

Appendix II

Five English inner cities

Birmingham (West Midlands)

Birmingham Inner Area (as defined by its Inner City Partnership) contains 14 wards and 280 000 people (1978 estimate), with a core area of particularly severe problems. A third of residents are non-white ethnic minorities (mostly West Indians and Asians). The West Midlands are traditionally dependent on the motor industry, and the inner area, containing 80% of the city's total employment, has lost jobs mainly in this and related industries (vehicles, metal, mechanical and electrical engineering).

Main inner city policy initiatives: Saltley Community Development Project, Small Heath Inner Area Study, and Birmingham Inner City Partnership. The sociological research of Rex & Moore in Sparkbrook was influential in theories of race and housing in the 1960s. Birmingham City Council, the largest district authority in England, has a tradition of municipal enterprise, having the first Municipal Bank in the days when Joseph Chamberlain was mayor. It has been probably the most active authority in the country in slum clearance and redevelopment, and more recently in area improvement. The Inner City Partnership gave priority to Handsworth, Sparkbrook, Small Heath, and unused land east of the city centre. Also in the West Midlands conurbation, Wolverhampton is a programme authority, and Dudley has an enterprise zone.

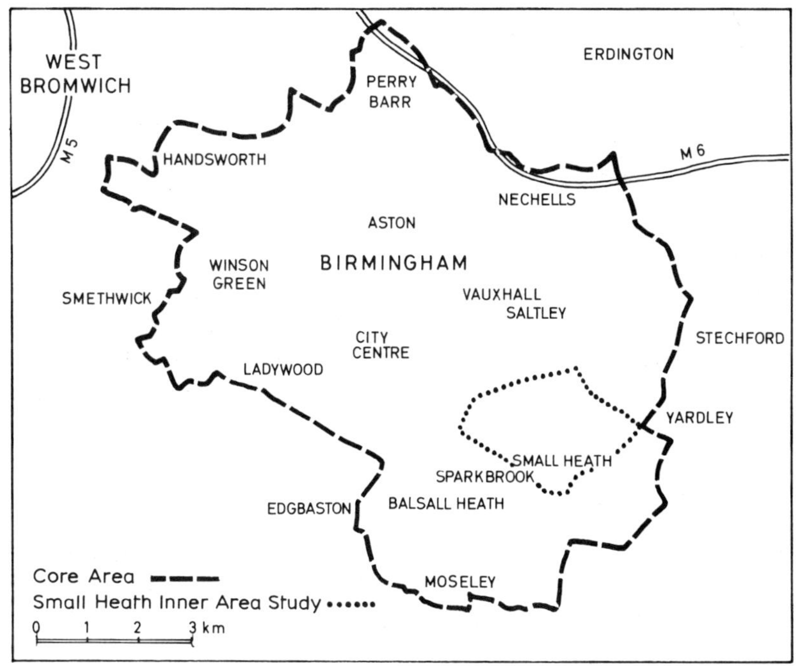

Birmingham Inner Area

Liverpool

Liverpool inner area has a population of about 300 000, including mixed ethnic minorities and a substantial element of Irish origin. The economic base of the city, its port and maritime trade, has been declining throughout the 20th century, from various factors (including the loss of Britain's overseas dependencies, the collapse of the Lancashire textile industry, and Britain's entry into the European Economic Community). The city council has been active in slum clearance and house-building, and recently in industrial promotion, but the loss of jobs to new towns and estates on the periphery has helped create the highest inner city unemployment levels in Britain, accompanied by widespread dereliction and under-investment. These contributed to the severe riots in the Toxteth area of the city in 1981.

Main inner city policy initiatives have included: Vauxhall Community Development Project, Shelter Neighbourhood Action Project in Granby, Liverpool Inner Area Study, Liverpool Inner City Partnership, Merseyside Development Corporation, and the Speke Enterprise Zone.

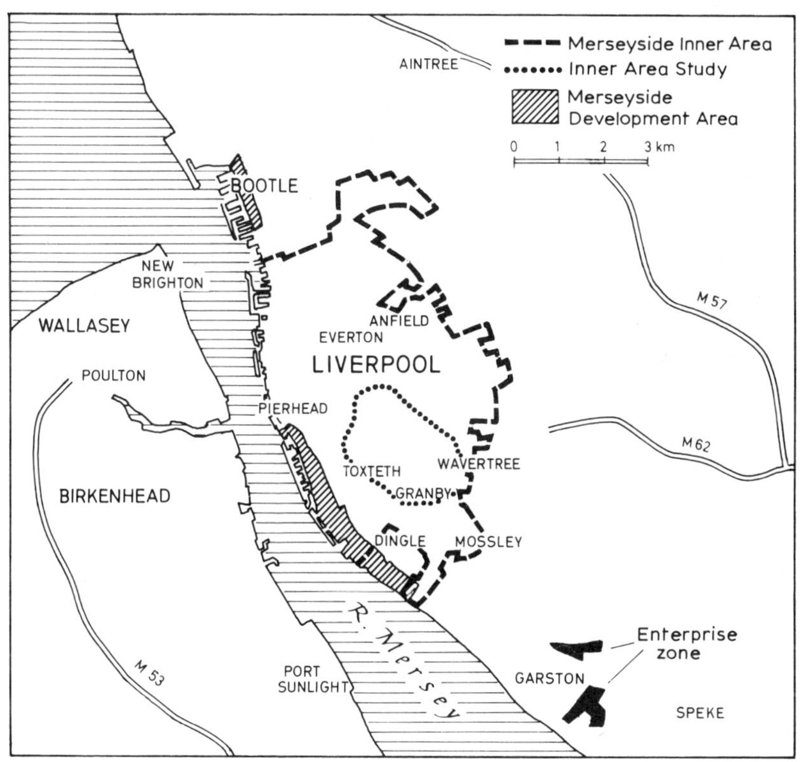

Merseyside Inner Area

London

London's inner city problems are concentrated in parts of the following boroughs: Camden, Hackney, Hammersmith, Haringey, Islington, Lambeth, Newham, Southwark, Tower Hamlets and Wandsworth. London has the largest population, of any British city, living in deprived inner areas (over two million), and has a large and varied ethnic minority population (including West Indian, Asian, African and Cypriot). Inner city policy initiatives have included Community Development Projects in Canning Town (Newham) and Newington (Southwark), the Stockwell Inner Area Study, Inner City Partnerships in Lambeth, Hackney-Islington (and for a time Docklands), the Isle of Dogs Enterprise Zone and the Docklands Development Corporation.

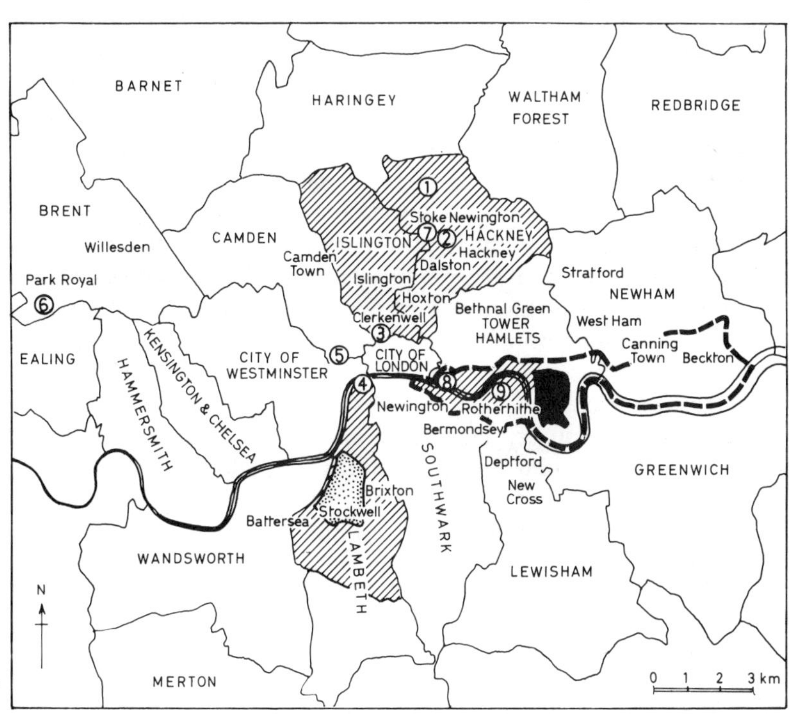

London's Inner Areas

Key

- London Borough boundaries
- Stockwell Inner Area Study
- Inner City Partnership areas
- Dockland Development Area
- Enterprise Zone

The London Boroughs are shown in capital letters

Inner city projects (see Appendix III)

1. Abney Park Cemetery
2. Bootstrap Enterprises and Centerprise Publications
3. Clerkenwell Workshops
4. Coin Street site
5. Covent Garden
6. Park Royal Enterprise Trust
7. Rio Cinema
8. St Katherine's Dock
9. Surrey docks

Manchester

The inner city problems of the Greater Manchester conurbation are more geographically widespread than elsewhere, in a number of authorities, formerly country boroughs, but now districts within the Greater Manchester Metropolitan County: Manchester, Salford, Oldham, Rochdale, Bolton, Stockport, etc. The main inner city areas (as defined by the Inner City Partnership) comprise 18 wards in Manchester City and 8 in Salford, with a combined population of 345 000 (1976 estimate). Historically the conurbation has strong links with Merseyside, and the dominant industry is textiles, which was vitally important to Britain's Empire in the 19th century, but has declined throughout the 20th, with a particularly high rate of family firm closures in recent years. The ethnic minority population is small compared with other inner cities.

Main inner city policy initiatives have included: Clarksfield (Oldham) Community Development Project, Deeplish (Rochdale) housing area improvement study, Crawford Street (Rochdale) Industrial Improvement Area, Manchester-Salford Inner City Partnership, Trafford Park Enterprise Zone, Stockport Economic Enterprise Area, and Bolton and Oldham programme authorities.

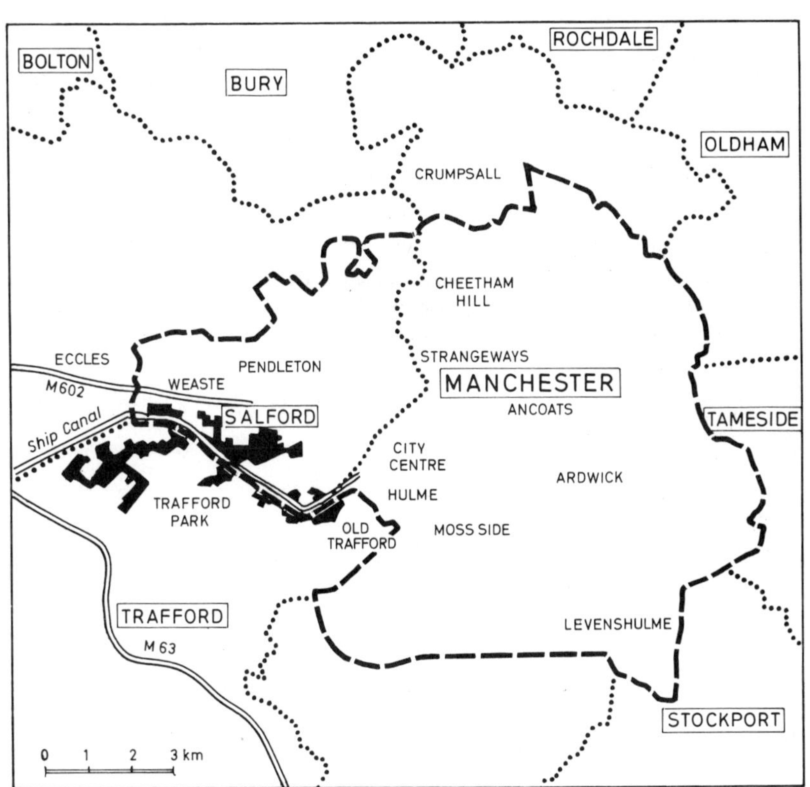

Manchester Inner Area

Key

Inner Area boundary

Metropolitan district boundaries

Enterprise zone

Newcastle

Inner city problems are spread along both banks of the River Tyne, and on Wearside, but are concentrated in Newcastle and Gateshead. The traditional economic base, ship-building and heavy industry, has been declining throughout the 20th century, and the area has chronically high unemployment (the Jarrow marchers in 1930 came from Tyneside), in spite of high levels of government regional aid (one of Britain's first trading estates was the Team Valley project in 1936) and a vocal regional lobby.

Main inner city policy initiatives have included: Benwell Community Development Project, Newcastle-Gateshead Inner City Partnership, Green Lane Industrial Improvement Area, Newburn Enterprise Zone, and programme authorities in North and South Tyneside and Sunderland.

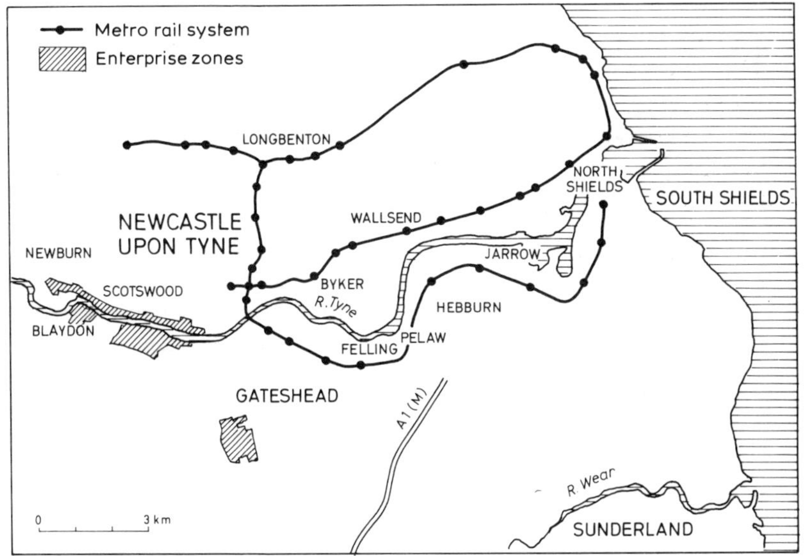

Newcastle Inner Area

Appendix III

Inner city regeneration projects

A number of projects are presented in this appendix which are intended to indicate the variety of activities which are being, or have been, undertaken in different inner city areas.

An address or reference is given for each project.

Abney Park Cemetery (Stoke Newington, London). Victorian cemetery used as an amenity area

This is a former country house estate which is still used as a non-denominational cemetery (graves include the Booth family of the Salvation Army), but is now neglected and overgrown. It was acquired by the London Borough of Hackney in 1978 from a private cemetery company for a nominal sum. Railings and buildings were restored from Operation Cleanup and Partnership funds, a monument survey was carried out and a guide prepared. It is used as a public open space and area of ecological significance. The address is: Stoke Newington High Street, London N16.

The Arnolfini Gallery (Bristol) was a Warehouse in a dock and is now converted to an arts centre and offices

Bush House is a 19th century tea warehouse in the City Docks. It is a listed building in a conservation area and was acquired in 1974 by a development company for their own offices (top four floors). It is shared with the Arnolfini Gallery, who have 20 000 square feet as a centre for visual and performing arts, with a bookshop, bar and restaurant, galleries, and a 200-seat performance area for cinema, dance and music. It is privately funded, with some grants from the Arts Council, Bristol City Council, etc. The gallery employs 27 full-time staff. The address is: St. Augustine's Reach, Bristol.

Black Road General Improvement Area (Macclesfield, Cheshire) is a self-help housing rehabilitation area

It is an area of workers' terraced houses intended for slum clearance, but the residents' action group showed that rehabilitation would be better and cheaper than redevelopment. The GIA declared that 34 houses should be rehabilitated in 1973. By 1975 these were substantially completed. The residents' association acted as its own general contractor, and the residents agreed minor alterations in property boundaries to allow communal accessways, car parking and environmental works. Macclesfield Borough Council gave full house improvement grants, loan facilities and legal aid, as well as relaxing planning and building controls (*Architect's Journal*, November 1975, pp. 995–1002).

Blackfriars Priory (Newcastle) is a historic building which has been restored to tourism and craft use

It is a largely complete 13th century Dominican Priory (Grade I listed building) owned by Newcastle City Council, in the Newcastle Central Conservation Area. It was converted to a craft centre and shop (Blackfriars Craftworkers Trust), and a tourist interpretation centre with exhibition space and restaurant. Phase I was completed in 1976, Phase II in 1981. Finance was obtained from county and district councils, the Historic Buildings Council and the English Tourist Board. The address is: Stowell Street, Newcastle, Tyne-and-Wear.

Bootstrap Enterprises (Dalston, East London) is a workship for the unemployed

It grew out of community workers' experience with a co-operative housing association. It provides a training workshop for unemployed, particularly black school-leavers, and a seedbed workshop for potential small businesses. Training includes machine-knitting, soft toy making, macrame and jewellery-making. It was begun in temporary premises in 1978 and now shares premises with similar groups. It is managed as a limited liability company. It is financed by charities, the education authority, companies and takings. The office address is: 22 Font-hill Road, London N4.

Borough Road/Poulton Road Shopping Improvement Area (Wallasey, Merseyside) is a commercial improvement area formed as a result of the Inner Urban Areas Act 1978

The Metropolitan Borough of Wirral, concerned at the decline of shopping areas following slum clearance, declared this a Shopping Improvement Area, with environmental improvements and grants for structural and amenity works. Details may be obtained from the Director of Development, Metropolitan Borough of Wirral, Town Hall, Wallasey.

Capital Jobmates (London) is an advice service for young people on finding work

It is sponsored by the National Extension College in association with Capital Radio and financed by the Manpower Services Commission. It was begun in 1979 and uses promotion through local commercial radio, written material on interview techniques, further education opportunities, etc., and a telephone referral service. The address is: 42 Store Street, London WC1.

Centerprise Publications (Dalston, East London) is a publishing and bookselling project specializing in local working-class culture

Centerprise opened in 1971 as a community centre based on a general bookshop, coffee bar and meeting room, in an area previously without a serious bookshop. It began publishing reminiscences of working people, local history, poems and teaching materials (about thirty books 1972–7). It is financed by sales and some grants. The address is: 136–8 Kingsland High Street, London E8.

Clerkenwell Workshop (London) is a series of small workshops in a converted warehouse

It is a 19th century warehouse (5570 square metres) which was converted by a private company in 1977–78 into 3720 square metres of usable floorspace, subdivided into 125 workshops and employing over 300 people. The venture started with £12 000 working capital, and used income from early tenants to finance a phased conversion programme for a low capital cost of £18 per square metre. The originators of the project (Mike Franks and Ted Potts) later formed a group under the name Regeneration, and were invited to rehabilitate other factories in partnership with the Greater London Council (industrial homesteading). The address is: Clerkenwell Green Association Ltd., 33 St. John's Square, London EC1.

Coin Street redevelopment (South Bank, London) is a controversial redevelopment proposal

A 13-acre site near the National Theatre, it is a derelict wharf area of the South Bank on which major office development has been proposed. But it has been meeting with strong opposition from local community groups urging housing and community facilities as preferable alternatives for the site. Schemes by property development companies were rejected by the Secretary of State after a long public inquiry in 1980. New mixed development proposals (nearly a million square feet of offices, with shopping, industry, housing and leisure facilities) by Greycoat Commercial Estates are the subject of a planning inquiry (twice adjourned on procedural grounds at the request of community groups and local authorities). The Conservatives controlling the Greater London Council sold a key part of this site to developers shortly before losing power in the 1981 GLC elections. Details: technical press, e.g. *Estates Times*, *Planning Newspaper*.

The Covent Garden Action Area (London) is a phased revitalization of a historic area of central London

The area has mixed uses including the Royal Opera House, many small businesses, buildings left by the move of London's main flower and vegetable market to a new site at Vauxhall, 30 000 daily commuters and 2800 residents. Proposals for a large-scale redevelopment were revised in favour of a mixed rehabilitation and redevelopment scheme. It was declared a Greater London Council action area in the Greater London Development Plan (1973), with two conservation areas and an informal local plan prepared with full public participation (1974–6). The policy of mixed use was intended to retain and promote the character of the area, with emphasis on flats, shops and light industry. Existing residents were safeguarded, and there was a priority on the rehabilitation of housing, especially through housing associations, with increased provision for families. The main feature of the action area is the creation of a tourism and entertainment centre: restoration and conversion of the listed Central Market building (built 1828–30) to a shopping arcade with restaurant (opened 1980), conversion of flower market to London Transport Museum, extension to Royal Opera House to provide ballet school etc. It was financed by county and district councils, the Historic Buildings Council, the English Tourist Board and many other agencies. Details: Greater London Council, County Hall, London SE1.

Glasgow Eastern Area Renewal is a comprehensive, co-ordinated regeneration project similar to Inner City Partnerships

It is a joint project between the Glasgow District Council, Strathclyde Regional Council, Scottish Special Housing Association, Scottish Development Agency and Greater Glasgow Health Board, with a governing committee chaired by the Secretary of State for Scotland. Its stated objectives are: to increase residents' ability to get jobs, generate employment, overcome residents' social disadvantages, improve environment, stem population decline and foster residents' confidence. £120 million were spent in 1976–80 on servicing industrial land, factories on SDA-owned land, a business centre in a former carpet factory, public housing completions, environmental improvements, with £7 million private investment in plant and machinery. (*Planning Newspaper*, 12 September 1980, p. 385).

The Hyson Green Workshops (Nottingham) are in a garage block on a council estate which was converted into small workshops

Two-storey 510-car garage block, built in 1968 within a 595-flat council estate, but vandalized and little used for its original purpose. On the initiative of the local tenants' association the ground floor was adapted to 28 small workshops (25–60 square metres) to create local employment and training opportunities. Finance was obtained from the Inner City Programme and European Social Fund. Details: Small Firms & Business Unit, Trent Polytechnic, Nottingham.

Impact Campaign (Greater Manchester) is a community-based environmental improvement programme

A variety of minor environmental schemes (repainting exteriors, garden improvement, waste land clearance and resurfacing, tree planting) was sponsored by the Greater Manchester County Council. It is administered through the Civic Trust for the North-West and 10 local committees, with a strong element of environmental education. Funds were given by the local authority and Operation Cleanup. Details: County Planning Officer, Greater Manchester County Council, County Hall, Piccadilly Gardens, Manchester M60 3HS.

Industrial Language Training (national) is a service providing English language teaching for ethnic minority workers

About 20 specialist units were established by local education authorities, mainly in inner city areas. When called in by firms, the units assess their communication needs in the workplace, and the levels of English spoken by ethnic minority workers. They provide language training courses (usually a minimum of 45–60 hours spread over 10–14 weeks), and train supervisory staff and trade unionists. The address is: National Centre for Industrial Language Training (NCILT), Recreation Road, Southall, Middlesex.

The Meanwood Valley Urban Farm (Leeds) is a city farm project

It is situated on a 13-acre site acquired by Leeds City Council for public open space, which has been leased to the urban farm management council (limited liability company and registered charity) since 1980 on a three-year lease. The uses include allotments, organic market gardening, livestock raising and grazing. Finance is from the Manpower Services Commission (nine jobs created), the Inner Area Programme and fund-raising. The address is: Sugarwell Road, Meanwood, Leeds 7, or City Farms Advisory Service, 15 Wilkin Street, London NW5 3WG.

The Merseyside Maritime Museum (Liverpool) is in a decayed dock area

The first phase comprises a visitor centre in the Old Pilotage Building at Pierhead, an outdoor display area, a shop and an exhibition area. It is partly funded by the Inner City Programme and Merseyside County Council. There are proposals for a major office and exhibition complex in the adjacent Liverpool Dock. The address is: Pierhead, Liverpool.

The Metro (Tyne-and-Wear) is a mass rapid transit system

It is a modification and improvement of the existing railway network linking most parts of the Tyne-and-Wear conurbation, with 4 passenger services, 34 route miles, 41 new stations and 4 interchanges (for transfer between rail, bus and car). It is the most recent major public transport investment in a British city. Phased opening is from 1980 onwards. Details: Tyne-and-Wear Passenger Transport Executive, Cuthbert House, All Saints, Newcastle.

Middlesbrough Enterprise Centre (Cleveland) is a terrace of workshops

They will be sited in a two-storey former biscuit factory in the St. Hilda's district of Middlesbrough. It will be converted into 15 small units with a communal workshop on the upper floor for testing proposals. It will be let under licence for up to 12 months, with equipment hired at an hourly rate, and floorspace for exhibition, meeting room and support services. Middlesbrough have already converted 30 terraced houses in Lorne and Howard Streets to 23 workshops, employing 84 people. The cost of the St. Hilda's project will be £1/4 million, from Inner Area Programme funds. (*Surveyor & Public Works Weekly*, 14 May 1981, pp. 8–9.)

Moseley Bog (Birmingham) was made into a schools wild-life conservation project

It is an area of bog and woodland surrounded by housing and playing fields. The natural environment for wild-life, including the rare wood horsetail, has been preserved. It was rediscovered in about 1977 and notified as a Site of Special Scientific Interest. Local school conservation corps carried out remedial works and a long-term management plan was prepared. Details: Nature Conservancy Council, Great Britain Headquarters, Belgrave Square, London SW1X 8PY.

Neighbourhood Energy Action (national) is a job creation scheme involving energy conservation projects

This is an extension of projects in Newcastle-upon-Tyne and Birmingham, initiated by Friends of the Earth, funded by the Manpower Services Commission's Community Enterprise programme, Inner City Programme and local authorities, under which temporary jobs were created insulating and draft-proofing several hundred inner city homes. It was extended by the National Council for Voluntary Organisations to a national programme to provide up to a thousand jobs, with training workshops, for energy conservation work in homes of the poor and elderly. The address is: NCVO, 26 Bedford Square, London W.1.

The Park Royal Enterprise Trust (North London) is a co-operative venture for improving the physical environment on London's largest industrial estate (30 000 employees)

It is a non-profit-distributing limited liability company which was created in 1980 and is supported by companies on the Park Royal

Estate (including Guinness, Heinz, Unigate and United Biscuits) and local councils through subscriptions and grants. The programme includes environmental improvements, advertisement hoardings to generate income, off-street parking arrangements, a newsletter and better arrangements for recruitment for companies' staff. It adopts a similar approach to Industrial Improvement Areas, but outside the *Inner Urban Area Act* framework. The address is: c/o United Biscuits Ltd, Waxlow Road, London NW10.

The Rio Cinema (Stoke Newington, East London) is an independent community cinema

When the original cinema closed, allegedly from vandalism and lack of customers, it was bought in 1979 by a co-operative, mainly of local community workers. The income from general release films subsidizes minority films and entertainments, live groups and other activities for the local community. Finance accrues from takings and some grants (e.g. Operation Cleanup to redecorate the exterior). The address is: 103 Kingsland High Street, London E8.

St. Katherine's Dock (East London) was a redundant dock area which has been converted into a business and recreation centre

The dock (about 12 hectares) was closed in 1968 and was bought from the Port of London Authority by the GLC. Taylor Woodrow, a major construction group, won a competition for development proposals, and leased the site. The development includes 730 dwellings (part council), the Tower Hotel (about 1600 bedspaces), the World Trade Centre (office, conference and exhibition facilities), Ivory House (19th century warehouse restored for residential and shopping use), Dickens Inn (timber-framed building relocated from inside a warehouse, and used as public house) and a Yacht Haven (marina, with historic vessel collection owned by the Maritime Trust). Part of the area was declared an outstanding conservation area. 1700 jobs are currently provided (excluding construction). The address is: St. Katherine's by the Tower, London.

The Woodlands Project (Glasgow) represents area improvement of housing and environment through residents' action

The project is based on an area of 19th century multi-storey tenement blocks (1500 dwellings), north of Glasgow city centre. In 1975 the Residents' Association with the City of Glasgow District Council prepared and implemented a programme of repair, external cleaning and environmental improvements on a block and area basis. Finance was obtained from grant aid and loans from the council. Details: Deputy Director of Administration, Glasgow District Council, City Chambers, George Square, Glasgow G2 1DU.

Index